A. Seth Pringle-Pattison

**Scottish Philosophy**

A Comparison of the Scottish and German answers to Hume

A. Seth Pringle-Pattison

**Scottish Philosophy**
*A Comparison of the Scottish and German answers to Hume*

ISBN/EAN: 9783337235390

Printed in Europe, USA, Canada, Australia, Japan

Cover: Foto ©Thomas Meinert / pixelio.de

More available books at **www.hansebooks.com**

Balfour Philosophical Lectures,
University of Edinburgh

# SCOTTISH PHILOSOPHY

A COMPARISON OF THE SCOTTISH AND
GERMAN ANSWERS TO HUME

BY

ANDREW SETH, M.A.

PROFESSOR OF LOGIC AND PHILOSOPHY
IN THE UNIVERSITY COLLEGE OF SOUTH WALES
AND MONMOUTHSHIRE

WILLIAM BLACKWOOD AND SONS
EDINBURGH AND LONDON
MDCCCLXXXV

*All Rights reserved*

TO

A. CAMPBELL FRASER, D.C.L., LL.D.

PROFESSOR OF LOGIC AND METAPHYSICS IN THE
UNIVERSITY OF EDINBURGH

THESE LECTURES ON SCOTTISH PHILOSOPHY

ARE GRATEFULLY AND AFFECTIONATELY

DEDICATED.

# PREFATORY NOTE.

In the winter of 1882-83 the question of establishing Lectureships in different departments of study was several times under the consideration of the Senatus of the University of Edinburgh. It appeared, however, that the Senatus had no legal right to use the University funds for such an experiment in intramural extension. In these circumstances, Mr A. J. Balfour, M.P., most generously offered to supply the endowment of the contemplated Lectureship in Philosophy for the first term of three years. The thanks of all friends of the University, and of philosophical students in particular, are due to Mr Balfour for this act of public spirit. My own are not less due for the personal kindness implied in the offer.

In consequence of my removal to Cardiff, these Lectures—forming the first course—were not delivered till towards the close of last session. They are now published substantially as they were then spoken. Some explanation of the reasons which dictated the choice of subject will be found in the opening of the first Lecture. The mode of treatment which I have followed I must leave to justify itself. It was the desire of the founder of the Lectureship, and it has been mine also, that the Lectures should be a contribution to philosophy, and not merely to the history of systems.

I hope, in a second course, to treat some aspects of the important question suggested at the close of the last Lecture.

ANDREW SETH.

UNIVERSITY COLLEGE, CARDIFF,
    *October* 1885.

# CONTENTS.

## LECTURE I.

### THE PHILOSOPHICAL PRESUPPOSITIONS: DESCARTES AND LOCKE.

PAGE

The choice of subject explained—Reid's view of Hume as the outcome of "the Cartesian system"—Subjectivity of Modern Philosophy—Defects of Descartes' starting-point—The two-substance doctrine—Failure of Cartesianism to explain Perception—Locke's version of the two-substance doctrine—Theory of Representative Perception—Ideas of primary and secondary qualities and of substances—Knowledge limited to our own ideas—Our consequent ignorance of Reality—Locke's account of Self and of God—His account of "sensitive knowledge"—Its limits unduly extended—Logical result of Locke's theory, . . . . . . . 1

## LECTURE II.

### THE PHILOSOPHICAL SCEPTICISM OF DAVID HUME.

Berkeley's criticism of Locke's second substance—Knowledge consists of ideas *and notions*—Reid's remarks on this addition to "the ideal system".—Two ways of developing Berkeley's philosophy—His hints of a rational idealism historically without influence—Hume's reduction of Locke and Berkeley to consistency—Perceptions divisible into impressions and ideas—Inference to a real cause of impressions unwarrantable—Every idea derived from some corresponding impression—Berkeley's (and Locke's) view of the arbitrary nature of natural connection stereotyped by Hume—Though conjoined, our particular perceptions remain entirely "loose"—Hume's account of space and time inconsistent with his sensational atomism—His further explanation of the *illusion* of causal connection, the *illusion* of a permanent world, the *illusion* of personal identity—His covert reintroduction of the Ego—His admissions in the Appendix—Necessity for a reconsideration of the two principles there laid down—Hume's real significance—Current misconceptions of his position, . 33

## LECTURE III.

### THOMAS REID: SENSATION AND PERCEPTION.

Reid answers Hume by attacking his presuppositions—Fresh analysis of Perception undertaken by Reid and Kant—Reid's account of Sensation and Perception in the 'Inquiry'—Perception involves "natural judgments"—Sensations as suggesting "signs"—Impossibility of deriving Space from feelings—Reid's error in admitting a separate knowledge of sensational signs—Reid's agreement with Kant (1) in vindicating Space as a percept impossible of derivation from sense; and (2) in making Judgment the unit of knowledge—Mutual implication of "natural judgments"—The meaning and limits of explanation, . . . 72

## LECTURE IV.

### REID AND KANT.

Misconceptions due to the unfortunate nomenclature adopted by Scottish philosophers — Comparison of Reid and Kant as to the *proof* which they offer of their " principles "—The transcendental deduction—Reid's defects here—The proof from the structure of language—General estimate of Reid's work—Kant's system as a whole—His conclusions depend on his previous admissions to Hume—Necessary connection, not being derivable from sense, must have a subjective source—Consequences of the consistent development of this view—Kant's unfaithfulness to his own principles—Statement of his conclusions—Useless invention of subjective machinery—The Categories already in things—The proper attitude towards Experientialism—Comparison of Kant with Reid in this respect, . . . . . . 106

## LECTURE V.

### THE RELATIVITY OF KNOWLEDGE: KANT AND HAMILTON.

The Kantian theory leaves us ignorant of reality—The doctrine of the Relativity of Knowledge as stated by Kant and Hamilton—Different lines of thought in the Relativistic argument—Argument from the numerical paucity and peculiar character of our avenues of knowledge—The argument rests on an unwarrantable isolation of the senses—Human reason as a peculiar psychical organisation—Abstract character of the doubt thus suggested—Argument from the relation essentially involved in all knowledge—This view refutes itself—Dependence of the doctrine on a false metaphysic of substance and quality—The logic of abstract identity—True use of the terms phenomenon and noumenon — "The Unknown and Unknowable"— Reason and Faith—Departure of Hamilton and Mansel from the catholic doctrine of Scottish Philosophy, 146

## LECTURE VI.

### THE POSSIBILITY OF PHILOSOPHY AS SYSTEM: SCOTTISH PHILOSOPHY AND HEGEL.

Is an absolute or completed system possible?—Hamilton's treatment of a similar question—His misconception of Hegel—General estimate of Hamilton—Prejudice against system to be avoided—The idea of system in Kant and Hegel—The Dialectic Method—True scope of Absolute Idealism—Misconceptions due to Hegel's mode of statement—The abstract universal no more real than the abstract particular—The Real as individual, and consequently inexhaustible—Unknown but not Unknowable—Knowledge and Faith—The completed system must remain for us an ideal, but an ideal in which we cannot but believe—The Natural Dualism of Scottish Philosophy not inconsistent with Absolute Idealism—Faults of German Idealism which might have been avoided by a national metaphysic, . 184

# SCOTTISH PHILOSOPHY.

## LECTURE I.

### THE PHILOSOPHICAL PRESUPPOSITIONS: DESCARTES AND LOCKE.

For the inauguration of a philosophical Lectureship—the first of its kind in a Scottish University—no subject appeared, for various reasons, more appropriate than a critical review of Scottish philosophy. Other grounds than the obvious one of national patriotism were present to my mind in choosing this subject; for at the first blush there is a savour of superfluity in discoursing on Scottish philosophy to a Scottish audience. This, however, is perhaps hardly so much the case as might be supposed. The thread of national tradition, it is tolerably well known, has been but loosely held of late by many of our best Scottish students of philosophy. It will hardly be denied that the philosophical productions of the younger generation of our University men are more strongly impressed with a German than with a native stamp. Against these productions we frequently hear the charge brought, that they represent an exotic culture, which is destined to pass like the fashion of a day. This new way of ideas labours, it is said, under a mortal weakness, in the cumbrous jargon in which its propositions are enunciated; and its representatives are taunted with a slavish adherence to set phrases and formulæ, and with a general inability to interpret and apply them in an intelligent and living way. Along with a certain amount of exaggeration, there is an admixture of truth in this account of the English and Scottish thinkers who derive their impulse from the German idealists. In spite of their large following—a following second only to that of Agnostic Empiricism—their doctrines have still a certain esoteric character. They appear to remain without influence upon the opposing school, and with but a limited influence upon the main course of English thought. Though the Idealists are constantly discharging their heavy artillery against the Empiricists and

Agnostics, the matter does not seem, somehow, to be brought to a vital issue; the cannonade appears to pass harmlessly over the enemy's head. Now, as nothing can be clearer, superficially at least, than the language in which Agnosticism lays down its positions, it is natural for candid critics to explain this lack of result, in part at all events, by pointing to the defects of exposition on the part of the Idealists. If this were the sole cause, it would be presumptuous in me to hope for better success than those who have gone before. But there can be no doubt, I think, that the difficulty which exists of coming to a common understanding is aggravated by the too exclusive attention which the idealistic school has been in the habit of bestowing upon a single group of foreign thinkers. I, for one, do not intend to deny that, of all modern philosophers, Kant and Hegel are those who deserve, and who at the same time demand, most study. But to this exclusiveness of spirit I think we may partly trace the isolation of parties which is one mark of the philosophic world at present. Some progress may be made, accordingly, towards bringing the opposing armies within fighting range of one another, if we turn our attention nearer home. With this idea the subject of these Lectures has been chosen.

Modern Empiricism builds upon Hume, and German philosophy claims to be, in the first instance, an *answer* to Hume. But there was another answer made to Hume—an answer made seventeen years before Kant's, in Hume's own country. Reid's answer, thought out at Aberdeen, and published in 1764, in the year of his translation to Glasgow, is but vaguely referred to in the histories of philosophy. The best of these are German; and for the Germans certainly Reid is not of decisive importance. In cosmopolitan influence, and, there is no injustice in adding, in speculative genius, he will not bear comparison for a moment with Kant. But that by no means proves that he may not be, for us in Scotland, a most valuable instrument in philosophising—perhaps, after long listening to German ways of putting things, as valuable an instrument as we could find. I mean, therefore, to try to seize the main drift of Reid's contention against Hume—a drift which seems frequently misunderstood—and to compare this "answer" with the answer of Kant and the amended answer of German Idealism since Kant's time. We shall thus see the mutual relations of the Scottish and the German answers, and be able to discover where the one is defective when judged by the standard of the other. As no one has pretended that Reid is unintelligible, the placing of his simple statement alongside of what people call the crabbed statement of German philosophy, may at least have the effect of elucidating the true bearings of the latter. Perhaps we may find even higher merits than this in Reid's straightforward and plain-spoken attempt. Such an undertaking, if carried out with any measure of success, cannot but lead to advantageous results, and must of necessity involve a treatment of some of the fundamental questions of philosophical debate.

For this purpose, it will be necessary to state, in as summary fashion as may be, the philosophical question which Reid set himself to answer, and the form in which he received it from the hands of his predecessor. If we do not see the problem, the solution offered will necessarily be without meaning for us; and if we do not see it as Reid saw it, we shall be unable to appreciate Reid's method of approaching it. Reid himself forces us to carry back our historical review as far as Descartes. In the dedication and introductory sections of the 'Inquiry into the Human Mind,' he speaks with as clear a consciousness as Kant of the new departure he is making in philosophy, and the antagonism it involves to all his predecessors. He passes in review Descartes, Malebranche, Locke, Berkeley, and Hume, exhibiting a very fair perception of the historic continuity of their speculations. The conclusion which he draws is, that "the system of all these authors is the same, and leads to scepticism."[1] Merging minor differences, he even goes the length of calling this common system by Descartes' name. "The system which is now generally received with regard to the mind and its operations, derives not only its spirit from Descartes, but its fundamental principles; and after all the improvements made by Malebranche, Locke, Berkeley, and Hume, may still be called *the Cartesian system.*"[2] The universal scepticism to which this philosophy has step by step, slowly but surely, led, is presumptive proof, he says again, "that Descartes' system of the human understanding, which I shall beg leave to call *the ideal system,* and which, with some improvements made by later writers, is now generally received, hath some original defect; that this scepticism is inlaid in it, and reared along with it; and, therefore, that we must lay it open to the foundation, and examine the materials, before we

[1] Works, p. 103 (ed. Hamilton).    [2] Ibid., p. 204.

can expect to raise any solid and useful fabric of knowledge on this subject."[1] In the Dedication he expresses the same thought in semi-Kantian phraseology, when he says that all the philosophical systems with which he was acquainted were built upon a certain "hypothesis"—a hypothesis of which he could find no solid proof, and which he therefore felt at liberty to discard. This hypothesis, which Reid felt it to be his mission to combat, has been already named. He generally speaks of it as "the ideal system," or "the theory of ideas"—that is to say, as he explains elsewhere, "the doctrine that all the objects of our knowledge are ideas in our own minds."[2] Let us now see in our own way, by reference to history, the full scope and meaning of Reid's contention.

It is usual to say that modern, as compared with ancient, philosophy has a predominatingly subjective character. And, though exceptions might be picked out on both sides, it is true that the stress laid upon the individual and the individual's consciousness is much more marked in modern than in ancient times. Whereas ancient philosophy chiefly investigated the nature of Being, modern philosophy has more and more

[1] Works, p. 103.   [2] Ibid., p. 283.

concentrated its attention upon the nature of Knowing. The most typical modern philosophers attack the former question only through the latter. This difference of point of view is evident even in the case of writers like Plato and Aristotle, whose works consist mainly in the discussion of ideas or conceptions. What is investigated is an objective ideal content,—the relation of Ideas to one another in an objective or cosmic system; the relation of the individual mind to this system, and the manner of the realisation of these Ideas in the individual consciousness, seemed to the ancients of less interest or importance. They have no definite answer to give to our modern questions, because, not separating man initially from the objective system they are considering, they do not see our difficulties, and naturally take for granted that he is somehow related to, and participant in, the universal reason. It is part both of the strength and the weakness of modern philosophy that it cannot satisfy itself so easily here.

Modern philosophy may be said to open, in Descartes, with a subjective note. This is true even of the emphatic announcement which he makes of his determination to cut himself adrift from the world of received opinion and custom, and to bring every belief before the bar of his individual reason. It has been pointed out a hundred times, how this is of the essence of the modern, the Protestant, the rational spirit; and it is not intended here to depreciate the importance of the step which Descartes took. But it is equally true that the individual, emptied in this way of all content, rational or otherwise, tends to become a mere atom or unqualified unit. He is thrust into a self-centred and merely self-dependent isolation from which it may become difficult to deliver him. For if a being be conceived as *merely* self-dependent—with no necessary relations beyond the relation to self—it is not easy to establish the existence of those relations at a later stage. This is exemplified in the further progress of Descartes' thought. The celebrated and much-praised starting-point of his system is in reality a false, or at all events an inadequate, foundation for philosophy; for it apparently affirms the independent existence of that which, when separated from the world, cannot be otherwise regarded than as a mere abstraction. "I exist;" but, as Descartes himself says, "how often? As often as I think. For perhaps it would even happen, if I should wholly cease to think, that I should at the same time altogether cease to be."[1] Thinking, then, is that whereby I exist; or, as Descartes expressed it, I am a being whose essence consists in thinking. But if this is so, it is necessary that the "I" should think *something*. As Kant afterwards expressed it, the unity of the Ego is not an abstract but a synthetic unity; it is realised, or is actual, only through a real or actual synthesis. In other words, a thinking being can become conscious of its existence and identity as a subject only by knowing objects—that is, a system of facts of some kind with which it is set in relation. Nor is it possible to defend Descartes by suggesting that the Ego, without going beyond the circle of its own individuality, may come to self-consciousness by thinking its own thoughts, recognised as different from one another, and in a sense distinguishable from the thinking Ego. This is, of course, the conception which lends colour to the ordinary forms of subjective idealism. But simply to place the whole system of facts within the individual consciousness in this way, is no solution of the real difficulty. Such an Ego, with its internal duality of subject and object, is itself "a little world," involving all the relations which, it has just been insisted, are essential to self-

[1] Second Meditation.

consciousness. It is not the bare unit which, having no relation to others, has no relation to self, and is therefore not a self at all.

As thinking, accordingly, in whatever form we take it, implies this duality, it must be fallacious to start as if one side of the antithesis could enjoy an independent existence. In terms of his own definition, already quoted, Descartes might have sought, in an analysis of the nature of thought, for some clue to the nature of the existence which he was entitled to attribute to the Ego. But, resting satisfied instead with the materialised conception of existence which is most natural to the human mind, he proceeds forthwith to define the Ego as a thinking substance. The stress falling ultimately on the "substance," the implicative nature of thought, which we have just been maintaining, is ignored, and thought becomes no better than any other quality of a thing, which belongs to the thing as its private property. Thus the thinking being is supposed to be shut up—like Lucretius's atoms, strong in solid singleness—within the circle of his own modifications or states.

Perception, or the knowledge by the Ego of a permanent world, is naturally the *crux* of a philosophy starting thus. Descartes' account is the result of his premature plunge into ontology, before the way was adequately prepared by a theory of knowledge. Enumerating perception as one species of thinking, he begins by treating it, not *as perception*, but simply as the presence of certain states of mind or mental modes. As he says in the opening of the Third Meditation: "The things which I perceive or imagine are perhaps nothing at all apart from me; but, in any case, I am assured that those modes of consciousness which I call perceptions and imaginations, in so far only as they are modes of consciousness, exist in me." But beyond their purely subjective or factual character as states of consciousness, our perceptions possess, according to Descartes, a representative character, as referred to objects beyond themselves—as images and effects, indeed, of things existing outside the thinking substance. It is only in this latter aspect—as symbolic of something beyond themselves—that they are *ideas* or *knowledge*, and that truth or falsity belongs to them. Otherwise they are merely internal *facts*, that come and go and have no meaning.[1] But if we start with mental modes unreferred, this subsequent reference of ideas to objects is evidently an inference which

[1] Cf. Bradley's Principles of Logic, Book I. chap. i.

may or may not be false. Nor does Descartes deny its problematical character. But he defends its truth, in the case of extension and its derivative notions, by reference to the truthfulness or trustworthiness of God. God cannot be supposed to deceive us in the case of ideas which are clearly and distinctly realised. Reid points out, however, the weakness of this argument; for, according to Descartes' principles, "our senses testify no more but that we have certain ideas, and if we draw conclusions from this testimony, which the premisses will not support, we deceive ourselves."[1] If we had a clear consciousness of extended substance as a permanent and relatively independent existence, the whole position would be changed; but, as it is, our fallacy lies at our own door. If we start with a self-contained subject, the time can never arrive when such a being would have any justification for referring its states beyond itself. Descartes, however, is here under the shadow of his own presuppositions. The abstraction of the thinking substance has its necessary counterpart in the abstraction of the extended substance. These are the two dead entities into which, as we may say, Descartes broke up the living whole of know-

[1] Works, p. 286.

ledge. Modern philosophy thus starts with two self-contained substances, each with its proper quality. The knowledge which the one acquires of the other is the result of the mechanical action of the other upon it. The ideas which represent material things are produced by the action of extended substance upon the thinking substance at the single point of location in the brain.

It would be needless to emphasise the difficulties which such a theory has to contend with. It is sufficient to point to the history of the Cartesian school for its immediate consequences. Occasionalism, which is simply logical Cartesianism, denies the possibility of any such interaction between the two substances as Descartes had admitted. Between mind and matter—thought and extension—an impassable gulf is fixed; the miraculously exerted will of God forms the only intermediary between the two worlds. Even in Spinoza, where the two finite substances pass into two sides of the divine nature, the existence of the two sides is empirically assumed, and their parallelism is also matter of dogmatic assertion. Malebranche, taking up the question from the point of view of knowledge, goes even further than Occasionalism. So far as the material world is concerned, the sole object of knowledge for

Malebranche is the <u>idea of extension</u> with its implications, or, as he calls it, intelligible extension. This, which is an ideal world, we know through our union with God, who illumines our minds. The existence of a real extended world, on the other hand—that is to say, Descartes' second substance—is not <u>known</u> at all, but is <u>believed</u> by Malebranche on grounds of supernatural revelation. In other words, it is maintained that our clear and distinct ideas do not, as Descartes had said, ground any inference to a non-ideal archetype or cause.

In English philosophy we can trace on a larger scale the evolution and self-refutation of the <u>two-substance doctrine</u> and the complementary theory of <u>Representative Perception</u>. To it, then, we now turn.

It was Locke who made the terms and distinctions of modern philosophy current coin in England. Locke's philosophy is also peculiarly interesting, because in it "the <u>theory of ideas</u>" is seen just detaching itself, as it were, from the groundwork of common-sense and ordinary belief. Analysis has only begun to do its work, and as yet we are but a single remove from the consciousness of the ordinary man. The account given of the human understanding commends itself as eminently credible, and not even very new. Only on looking closer do we see how far the first step in analysis has in reality carried us, and to what strange conclusions it has occasionally conducted Locke. In the course of his theorising, as Reid truly remarks, "the author is led into some paradoxes, although in general he is not fond of paradoxes."[1] Let us look, then, with some care at the main features of the system elaborated in the Essay.

First, then, it may be noted that Locke took for granted the independent existence, on the one hand, of a system of material substances, which we may call the material world; and, on the other hand, of a number of separate minds or substances with the power of thinking. He also took for granted the interaction of these substances, supposing that, in perception, the material object perceived communicates a knowledge of itself to the perceiving mind by a species of impact, or mechanical impression. "Bodies," he says, "produce ideas in us . . . manifestly by impulse, the only way which we can conceive bodies operate in."[2] So much he found warrant for alike in the common consciousness of mankind, and in the philosophy with which he was

[1] Works, p. 294.   [2] Essay, ii. 8, 11.

acquainted, whether the Aristotelianism of the schools or the new philosophy of Descartes. As regarded the nature of mind or the thinking substance, he declined to commit himself on the question of its material or immaterial nature; but he was explicit as to its characterlessness previous to experience. Whether material or immaterial, the mind may be compared to "white paper, void of all characters, without any ideas."[1] On this white paper or *tabula rasa* external things leave their mark or impression, in the shape of what Locke calls "ideas of sensation." Or, adopting another metaphor, Locke tells us that "the senses at first *let in particular ideas*, and furnish the yet empty cabinet."[2] "External and internal sensations are the only passages that I can find of knowledge to the understanding. These alone, as far as I can discover, are the windows by which light is let into this dark room. For methinks the understanding is not much unlike a closet wholly shut from light, with only some little opening left to let in external visible resemblances or ideas of things without."[3] Perception, he puts it again, is "the inlet of all knowledge into our minds;" or, more properly, "of all the materials of it"[4]—the remaining operations of

[1] Essay, ii. 1, 2.    [2] I. 2, 15.    [3] II. 11, 17.    [4] II. 9, 15.

the mind being merely to compare and variously combine or separate the simple ideas thus passively received. "All that man can do is either to unite them together, or to set them by one another, or wholly separate them."[1]

Secondly, as implied in some of the passages just quoted, Locke took for granted, in regard to the knowledge which the mind has of the world, the theory of Representative Perception which he found current in the schools. "It is evident," he says, "the mind knows not things immediately, but only by the intervention of the ideas it has of them."[2] All our knowledge, he repeats, consists "in the view the mind has of its own ideas."[3] "Since the mind, in all its thoughts and reasonings, hath no other immediate object but its own ideas, which it alone does or can contemplate, it is evident that our knowledge is only conversant about them."[4] This is what Reid means by "the common theory of ideas," or "the ideal system." To each idea there corresponds some modification of the material thing of which it is an idea; but the latter—the modification or property of the thing—is not itself known to us. We know only the idea which it causes. The name "idea" being

---

[1] Essay, ii. 12, 1.      [2] IV. 4, 3.
[3] IV. 2, 1.      [4] IV. 1, 1.

thus restricted to "whatsoever the mind perceives in itself, or is the immediate object of perception, thought, or understanding,"[1] its correlative or cause in the material substance receives from Locke the name "quality." A quality in an object is "the power to produce any idea in my mind." "Thus," he adds, "a snowball having the power to produce in us the ideas of white, cold, and round, the powers to produce those ideas in us, as they are in the snowball, I call 'qualities'; and as they are sensations or perceptions in our understandings, I call them 'ideas.'"[2] Strictly speaking, however, we have no knowledge of the qualities as qualities; we merely infer some correlative of our ideas. For ideas are a kind of *tertium quid*—an intermediary between the mind and things, which cuts us off from a knowledge of the actual things. They are like images projected upon a mental screen; and the screen is the limit of our vision, immediate knowledge being what the mind "perceives *in itself*." We cannot see, therefore, what is behind the screen and throws the image. Hence, Locke immediately apologises for his loose way of speaking, and adds that, if he sometimes speaks of ideas as in the things themselves, he "would be under-

[1] Essay, ii. 8, 8.      [2] II. 8, 8.

stood to mean those qualities in the objects which produce them in us." [1]

Some of our ideas are "representative," in the strict sense of the word; that is to say, "the ideas or perceptions in our minds" exactly resemble the "modifications of matter in the bodies that cause such perceptions in us." These Locke calls primary qualities; and he enumerates as such solidity, extension, figure, and mobility, which may be reduced to solidity or impenetrability and extension with its derivative qualities. In the case of these, the idea is simply the duplicate—the accurate image—of the quality. The "patterns" of the primary qualities "do really exist in the bodies themselves." [2] But in the case of such ideas as those of colour, taste, sound, &c., only an uninstructed mind can suppose that there is anything like our ideas existing in the bodies themselves. The qualities of body which produce ideas of this sort Locke calls secondary qualities. He points out that they are in truth "nothing in the objects themselves but powers to produce various sensations in us" by different modifications of their primary qualities—that is, by a certain "bulk, figure, texture, and motion of their insensible parts." [3] To take an illustration: "A

[1] Essay, ii. 8, 8.   [2] II. 8, 15.   [3] II. 8, 10.

piece of manna of a sensible bulk is able to produce in us the idea of a round or square figure; and, by being removed from one place to another, the idea of motion. This idea of motion represents it as it really is in the manna moving; a circle or square are the same, whether in idea or existence, in the mind or in the manna; and thus both motion and figure are really in the manna, whether we take notice of them or no: this everybody is ready to agree to. Besides, manna, by the bulk, figure, texture, and motion of its parts, has a power to produce the sensations of sickness, and sometimes of acute pains or gripings, in us. That these ideas of sickness and pain are not in the manna, but effects of its operations upon us, and are nowhere when we feel them not; this also every one readily agrees to." In exactly the same way, sweetness and whiteness "are not really in manna;" they are "but the effects of the operations of manna by the motion, size, and figure of its particles on the eyes and palate."[1] In short, as regards the secondary qualities: "Take away the sensation of them; let not the eyes see light or colours, nor the ears hear sounds; let the palate not taste, nor the nose smell; and all colours, tastes, odours, and sounds, as they are

[1] Essay, ii. 8, 18.

such particular ideas, vanish and cease, and are reduced to their causes — *i.e.*, bulk, figure, and motion of parts."[1]

But if our ideas are to give a full representation or account of the material world, they must embrace not only ideas of the primary and secondary qualities, but also ideas of the substances to which these qualities belong. Locke has assumed the existence of material substances, and therefore he recognises the reasonableness of this demand. But the idea of substance costs him much trouble. "We have no such clear idea at all,"[2] he says; but the mind, taking notice that a certain number of its ideas go constantly together, falls into the habit of calling the combination by a single name. "Not imagining how these simple ideas can subsist of themselves, we accustom ourselves to suppose some substratum wherein they do subsist, and from which they do result; which, therefore, we call substance."[3] The word signifies no more than this "supposition of we know not what support of such qualities which are capable of producing simple ideas in us." Locke takes the examples of "a man, horse, gold, water," and appeals to every one's own experience whether he has any other clear idea of these substances

---

[1] Essay, ii. 8, 17.    [2] I. 4, 18.    [3] II. 23, 1.

farther than of certain simple ideas coexisting together. "Only," he adds, "we must take notice that our complex ideas of substances, besides all these simple ideas they are made up of, have always the confused idea of something to which they belong, and in which they subsist; and therefore, when we speak of any sort of substance, we say it is a thing having such or such qualities."[1] To sum up the difficulty, the idea of substance is, according to his own explicit statement, one "which we neither have nor can have by sensation or reflection;"[2] yet external and internal sensation, as we have seen, are maintained by Locke to be "the only passages that [he] can find of knowledge to the understanding." But in spite of this embarrassing result as regards the *idea* of substance, Locke never wavered for an instant in his belief that substances exist. When taken to task by the Bishop of Worcester because, by his new way of ideas, he had "almost discarded substance out of the reasonable part of the world," he was able to answer complacently that "the being of things in the world depends not on our ideas."[3] Locke stood too firmly rooted in the everyday practical consciousness of mankind to be disturbed in his assumptions by the

[1] Essay, ii. 23, 3.   [2] I. 4, 18.   [3] First Letter.

negative results to which his own theory seemed to be leading.

These results come most clearly to light in the Fourth Book of the Essay, which deals specifically with 'Knowledge.' As Reid shrewdly remarks, "a great part of that Book is an evident refutation of the principles laid down in the beginning of it."[1] For knowledge being, according to Locke, only "conversant about our ideas"—being defined, in fact, as the perception of the agreement or disagreement of any of our ideas—it follows that we have no knowledge whatever of reality or existence, which is something different from ideas. But Locke breaks through his own definition at three points. *First*, in reference to his own substantial existence. Of this he says, following Descartes almost verbally, that he has an intuitive knowledge. "We perceive it so plainly and so certainly, that it neither needs nor is capable of any proof. . . . In every act of sensation, reasoning, or thinking, we are conscious to ourselves of our own being; and in this matter come not short of the highest degree of certainty."[2] *Secondly*, in regard to the existence of God. Knowledge of this may be reached, according to Locke, by a process of *a posteriori* reasoning,

[1] Works, p. 432.      [2] Essay, iv. 9, 3.

starting from the intuitively known fact of my own existence. This is demonstrative knowledge; and if the chain of proof is cogent, it stands on the same level of certainty as intuitive knowledge.[1] It does not belong to our purpose to dwell further at present on these instances of knowledge of existence admitted by Locke. It is enough, in the meantime, to point out that the knowledge of Self thus assumed is at variance with the principles of his own philosophy. For Self is not maintained to be an idea either of sensation or reflection; it is a consciousness which accompanies "every act of sensation, reasoning, or thinking." The admission of such an element in knowledge points, therefore, to the inadequacy of any theory which makes knowledge consist entirely of simple or particular ideas variously combined. The *third* point at which Locke breaks down his definition of knowledge is in what he calls sensitive knowledge. "The knowledge of the existence of any other thing [beyond Self and God] we can have," says Locke, "only by sensation."[2] Now this is of course true, if it merely means that we can become aware of the existence of external things only through the process of perception. But it hardly appears

[1] See Essay, iv. 10, 1-6.   [2] IV. 11, 1.

how this knowledge of existence is contained in Locke's ideas of sensation. Such ideas are simple; they are themselves, and in consistency they testify only to their own existence. Granted that I know my own ideas of sensation, what advance have I made, on Locke's principles, to a knowledge of the real objects—their external causes and correlates? Locke himself admits that the two cases stand upon a different platform of certainty. The knowledge of the idea is intuitive knowledge; "but whether there be anything more than barely that idea in our minds, whether we can thence certainly infer the existence of anything without us which corresponds to that idea, is that whereof some men think there may be a question made."[1] But he gets over the doubt by a reference to the difference between ideas of sensation and the ideas of memory or of dreams. He admits, however, that, though "going beyond bare probability," sensation is not to be placed on the same level of certainty as the kinds of knowledge already mentioned (intuitive and demonstrative). Sensitive knowledge "passes under the name of knowledge;"[2] it is "an assurance that deserves the name of knowledge;"[3] and, as Locke character-

[1] Essay, iv. 2, 14.  [2] IV. 2, 14.  [3] IV. 11, 3.

istically observes, it is "folly to expect demonstration in everything."[1] "This certainty is as great as our happiness or misery, beyond which we have no concernment to know or to be."[2]

In any case, this <u>sensitive</u> knowledge could only be, as Locke puts it, a knowledge "that something doth exist at that time without us which causes that idea in us"[3]—that is to say, an indefinite reference to *some* cause, not a definite reference to an individually determinate thing. But it does not appear how even this amount of knowledge is contained in Locke's simple ideas. If they do carry with them a causal reference to an independently existing substance, that is a fact which ought to be most carefully noted in our analysis of perception ; for it at once disposes of the supposition that knowledge is built up entirely of independent sensational units called <u>simple ideas</u>. Locke himself did not follow out this consequence, mainly because he was so sure of the two-substance doctrine which he assumes throughout, partly also because he imported the doctrine unwarrantably into the phraseology he employs. Thus, in one of the passages already referred to, he says: "There can be nothing

[1] Essay, iv. 11. 10.    [2] IV. 2, 14.    [3] IV. 11, 2.

more certain than that *the idea we receive from an external object* is in our minds; this is intuitive knowledge."[1] If this were true, all that he goes on to say about the inferior certainty of sensitive knowledge would be manifestly out of place. But, by his own admissions, it is only the existence of the idea in the mind, as a mental fact, that can be designated intuitive knowledge; and he has no right, therefore, to qualify the idea at this stage as an "idea which we receive from an external object."

Besides placing sensitive knowledge on a lower level as regards certainty, and admitting it, so to speak, only by courtesy to the title of knowledge, Locke proceeds to limit the range of this knowledge. It "extends as far as the present testimony of our senses, employed about particular objects that do then affect them, and no farther.[2] The present existence of certain particular ideas of sensation, therefore, or, on the testimony of memory, the past existence of such sensations at such and such a moment: that is all.[3] *Tecum habita, et nôris quam sit tibi curta suppellex.*

---

[1] Essay, iv. 2, 14.   [2] IV. 11, 9.

[3] "Concerning the existence of finite spirits, as well as several other things, we must content ourselves with the evidence of faith. . . . We have ground from revelation, and several other reasons, to believe with assurance that there are such

Locke's cloak is becoming very scanty—hardly sufficient for everyday needs. But there is no possibility of mistaking Locke on this point. He repeatedly insists that propositions about nature, if general, cannot be certain, and if certain, cannot be general. General propositions of whose truth we can be certain have to do exclusively with abstractions of our own making, as in the sciences of mathematics and morals. The ideas being there framed and defined by ourselves, we can of course draw consequences from them that will be universally true. But it is not so in matters of fact, where the collections of ideas we receive are not of our own framing, and where consequently, being ignorant of the constitution of the things which the ideas represent, and on which they depend, we do not know the actual connections of ideas or qualities. He suspects, accordingly, that "natural philosophy is not capable of being made a science. . . . Experiments and historical observations we may have, from which we may draw advantages of ease and health, and thereby increase our stock of conveniences for this life; but beyond this, I

---

creatures ; but, our senses not being able to discover them, we want the means of knowing their particular existences."—Essay, iv. 11, 12.

fear our talents reach not, nor are our faculties, as I guess, able to advance."[1] "All general knowledge," he repeats and emphasises, "lies only in our own thoughts, and consists barely in the contemplation of our own abstract ideas."[2] Having reached this conclusion, Locke proceeds to remark in his pithy English that "our knowledge being short, we want something else."[3] This "something else" he calls Judgment, which is defined as "the presuming things to be so without perceiving it." It may be, as Locke is fond of reminding us, that this certainty is sufficient for our happiness or misery, and for the business we have to do here; but it is evident, at least, that by far the greater part of what is ordinarily spoken of as human knowledge is enveloped, according to Locke's theory and his own express statement, in "the twilight of probability."[4]

It only requires to be noted further, that in the foregoing account Locke allows himself more licence than he is fairly entitled to. In speaking of the present testimony of our senses, he extends this testimony so as to make it cover the

---

[1] Essay, iv. 12, 10.
[2] IV. 6, 13. See also iv. 6, 16; iv. 9, 1; iv. 12, 7, &c.
[3] IV. 14, 1.   [4] IV. 14, 2.

perception of "such collections of simple ideas as we have observed by our senses to be united together"—such a collection, for example, as is wont to be called "man." But if <u>simple ideas or detached sensational atoms</u> are the sole materials of knowledge, each of these must be impressed upon us in its own moment of time; and the testimony of the senses to an existent reality holds only for that moment. When we have passed on to the second idea of the collection, the testimony of the senses holds for the second but no longer for the first. We are never, therefore, in the possession of such testimony to the existence of a real object combining in itself the qualities represented by such a series of ideas as is implied in the collections instanced.

The logical consummation of Locke's theory thus leaves him nothing but the <u>unrelated atoms of sense</u>, the simple or particular ideas with which he set out as the materials of all our knowledge. But this consummation is evaded by Locke himself, partly through open departure from his own principles, and partly through the looseness of his language. The Ego we have seen him simply transfer from Descartes' system to his own. Other importations are covered by the ambiguity of his terminology, more particularly by the liberal scope assigned to the term sensation. It is his usual practice, for example, to interchange "sensation" and "perception" at will; to treat space as a simple idea—*i.e.*, as a sensation of touch or of sight; and to speak vaguely of "power" or cause as a simple idea received both from sensation and reflection. It was great part of the work of the philosophers and psychologists who followed Locke to define these terms more exactly. Just in proportion as they did so, the Lockian theory became more consistent in their hands, but at the same time very much less plausible than it had been in Locke's. It becomes our duty to describe shortly the process by which Locke's theory passed — in virtue of elements initially omitted—by a perfectly logical and inevitable development, into the thorough-going Scepticism which roused Reid, like Kant, from his dogmatic slumber.

## LECTURE II.

#### THE PHILOSOPHICAL SCEPTICISM OF DAVID HUME.

We saw in the first lecture how Reid recognised Hume's scepticism as the necessary issue of principles inherent in the modern or Cartesian philosophy, and, more particularly, as the outcome of the avowed principles of Locke. This led us to review the philosophical presuppositions, as they exist in the systems of Descartes and Locke. We have now to consider the final form of "the theory of ideas" in Hume. A few words on Berkeley will suffice by way of transition and introduction; for we have only to do with Berkeley here so far as he puts his hand to the lever in the work of disintegration referred to at the close of last lecture.

Berkeley's first task was to expose the baseless, useless, and self-contradictory character of the unperceived absolute matter of Locke and other philosophers. And here, as Reid says, Berkeley's system follows from Locke's by very obvious consequence; "in the new philosophy, the pillars by which the existence of a material world was supported were so feeble that it did not require the force of a Samson to bring them down."[1] Locke's assumption of a resemblance between the primary qualities and the ideas which they cause in us was, even on his own principles, so perfectly arbitrary, that the knowledge we have of external things had dwindled down under his hands, as we have seen, to the momentary consciousness of "some exterior cause."—"something at that time really existing without us which doth affect our senses." But if this is so, what warrant have we for supposing that this cause is material substance? We mean by that phrase either — as ordinary men — the so-called primary qualities, *i.e.*, a collection of certain ideas; or we mean—as philosophers — the substance supporting these qualities, *i.e.*, something we know not what. In the first case, it is absurd to speak of the ideas which constitute matter as existing otherwise than in a mind; in the second case, we have need to consider what we mean by causality, before we

[1] Works, p. 282.

attribute it to an abstraction of our own making. On Lockian principles, Berkeley thus resolves matter into simple ideas *plus* the notion of some cause. The <u>ideas</u> or <u>sensations</u>, strictly mind-dependent in their nature, are variously clustered together, and, as such clusters, constitute "<u>things</u>." And as they, moreover, succeed or introduce one another in an orderly and coherent way, we gradually learn to recognise constant conjunctions, to which we give the name of laws of nature.

How closely this reproduces Locke on the one hand, and how nearly it anticipates Hume on the other, hardly needs to be pointed out. In fact, Berkeley hardly professes to reach his position by a process of argument at all. He simply states it. "Some truths there are so near and obvious to the mind, that a man need only open his eyes to see them." Reid points out that the whole theory is virtually contained in the opening sentences of the 'Principles of Human Knowledge': "It is evident to any one who takes a survey of the objects of human knowledge, that they are either ideas actually imprinted on the senses; or else such as are perceived by attending to the passions and operations of the mind" [Locke's simple ideas of sensation and reflection—the materials of all our knowledge]; or lastly, ideas formed by help of memory and imagination—either compounding, dividing, or barely representing those originally perceived in the aforesaid ways" [Locke's complex ideas, combinations of the simple ones by the same mechanical methods here enumerated]. Reid remarks that, if the identification of objects of knowledge with ideas be admitted, "Berkeley's system is impregnable."[1] But it was precisely the issue raised by Reid, in reference to the Cartesian system generally, that perception is in no case to be identified with relationless impressions, or any combination of them, but involves other elements or principles which alone give it objective significance.

In the remainder of his system, Berkeley follows Locke in his assumptions rather than in the strict logic of his theory. He reaches his construction of the universe really through unfaithfulness to their common principles. At one stage in his career, it is true, in the early days of the Commonplace Book, Berkeley seemed inclined to follow out his analysis to the same conclusions as Hume. "The very existence of ideas constitutes the soul. Mind is a congeries of perceptions. Take away perception, and you take away mind.

[1] Works, p. 283.

Put the perceptions, and you put the mind."[1] But although _ideas_ (according to the definition common to himself and Locke) exhaust the _objects_ of knowledge, he everywhere adds to them, in his published works, what he calls a _notion_ of self. And from this he passes, by _analogy_ and by the help of the _principle of causality_, to other spirits, and, in particular, to the Divine Spirit, who is the sustaining and co-ordinating principle of the Berkeleian universe. Berkeley has the merit, as compared with Locke, of making this additional postulate consciously, and putting it in the forefront of his system. "Thing or Being," he says, "is the most general name of all; it comprehends under it two kinds entirely distinct and heterogeneous, and which have nothing common but the name—viz., Spirits and Ideas. The former are active, indivisible substances; the latter are inert, fleeting, or dependent beings, which subsist not by themselves, but are supported by or exist in minds or spiritual substances. . . . We may not, I think, strictly be said to have an _idea_ of an active being or of an action, although we may be said to have a _notion_ of them. I have some knowledge or notion of my mind and its acts about ideas, inasmuch as I know or understand what is

[1] Life and Letters of Berkeley (Clarendon Press), p. 438.

meant by these words. . . . It is also to be remarked that, all *relations* including an <u>act of the mind</u>, we cannot so properly be said to have an <u>idea</u>, but rather a <u>notion</u> of the relations and habitudes between things."[1] And elsewhere he combats "the opinion that <u>spirits</u> are to be known after the manner of an <u>idea</u> or <u>sensation</u>" as having given rise to many absurd and heterodox tenets, and much scepticism about the nature of the soul."[2] He himself holds it to be "evidently absurd" that the "<u>substance</u> which supports or perceives <u>ideas</u> should itself be an idea or like an idea"; and "to expect that by any multiplication or enlargement of our faculties we may be enabled to know a spirit as we do a triangle, seems as absurd as if we should hope to see a sound."[3]

Reid at once put his finger on the important deviation of principle which these passages contain. "This account of ideas," he says, "is very different from that which Locke has given. In his system we have no knowledge where we have no ideas. Every thought must have an idea for its immediate object. In Berkeley's, the most important objects are known without ideas." Whether, continues Reid, he "foresaw the consequences that

[1] Principles, sections 89 and 142.   [2] Section 137.
[3] Sections 135 and 142.

may be drawn from the system of ideas, taken in its full extent, and which were afterwards drawn by Mr Hume, I cannot pretend to say. . . . However this may be, if there be so many things that may be apprehended and known without ideas, this very naturally suggests a scruple with regard to those that are left; for it may be said, If we can apprehend and reason about the <u>world of spirits</u>, without ideas, is it not possible that we may apprehend and reason about a <u>material world</u>, without ideas?"[1] In another passage, he expressly attributes Berkeley's action here to "his great aversion to Scepticism." "In order to avoid Scepticism, he fairly starts out of the Cartesian system, without giving any reason why he did so in this instance, and in no other."[2] Whether unexceptionably expressed or not, the criticism urged here by Reid is a true one, and goes to the heart of the matter. If the existence of ideas involves, in one aspect, a permanent combining principle called <u>Self</u>, which is not an idea or impression, may not a similar principle or similar principles be involved in that coherence of the ideas which constitutes the <u>material universe</u>? Does not the perception of ideas, on Berkeley's own theory, depend on the

[1] Works, p. 288.   [2] Ibid., p. 207.

unacknowledged presence of such an element? Evidently it does; Berkeley's theory of divine causation and intelligible connection is entirely dependent on such a principle. Quite as much as Locke, he takes the ideas of sense, not as mere ideas, but as ideas referred to each other and to some cause—though the cause assigned by the two philosophers is different. It is not ideas *per se*, but ideas as interpretable, as significant of a permanent order, that supply him with the foundation for his system.

Indeed, if Berkeley had set himself to an analysis of the elements which his constructive theory involved over and above sense-ideas, and not derivable from them, there might perhaps have been no Hume; for we should have had, at one step, a rational instead of a sensational idealism. What is this explicit addition of intellectual notions to the data of sense but, in germ, Reid's principles of common-sense, or Kant's system of the categories? If Berkeley had asked himself what extent he was prepared to give to his afterthought that relations, as involving a mental activity, are therefore to be distinguished from the ideas or data of mere sense, and if he had at the same time continued his analysis of such supposed data into their primitive elements, he might have found that the relations tended to swallow up the ideas, to such an extent that it ultimately became impossible to point to anything at all that could be considered as a mere "given," as a relationless or atomic datum. For spatial <u>distance</u> and <u>temporal succession</u> are both relations; and can we have an idea not so qualified? So is also that relation of <u>sign</u> and <u>thing signified</u>, which constitutes for Berkeley physical causation, and which is the basis of the interpretability of the universe. If a sensation is not referred to something, what can be said of it? In what does its existence consist? Berkeley would have been ready to admit that it must at least be referred to me as mine—that this relation, therefore, at the lowest is necessary to render it knowable. But the unknowableness of sense-atoms or mere data, except as somehow related to one another, had not forced itself upon him at the date of his epoch-making works. He says unhesitatingly in the 'Principles'[1] that "<u>relations</u> are distinct from the <u>ideas</u> or <u>things related</u>, inasmuch as the latter may be perceived by us without perceiving the former." He is thinking, of course, of the undoubted truth that we may first consider an object by itself, as we say, and then add to this

[1] Section 89.

survey a consideration of its relations to other things—to its environment, for example, or the past of which it is the outcome. But is the thing, as originally considered, absolutely without relations? On the contrary, it is simply impossible to consider anything in sheer isolation from its temporal and spatial environment; every quality which we recognise involves relations to other things, and it is as a complex of such relations that the "thing" in question receives its name and place in the universe. Berkeley had not carried his analysis as far as this when he wrote the 'Principles'; but in 'Siris' we find that he has left his early positions far behind him. "We know a thing," he says, "when we understand it; and we understand it when we can interpret or tell what it signifies. Strictly, the Sense knows nothing."[1] And, in words that almost recall Kant's often-quoted statement about the mutual dependence of sense and understanding, he says again: "As understanding perceiveth not, so sense knoweth not; and although the mind may use sense and fancy, as means whereby to arrive at knowledge, yet sense or soul, so far forth as sensitive, knoweth nothing."[2]

But 'Siris' was without influence upon English

[1] Section 253. [2] Section 305.

thought—at all events till the present generation, which has reaped the fruit of Professor Fraser's loving care. It is enough for us here, therefore, to recognise the fact that Berkeley's philosophy may be developed in two directions. Berkeley seems, as we have seen, to have recognised the inevitable consequences of mere Lockianism—I mean, of consistent adherence to "the ideal system"— and to have consciously shifted his ground in consequence. He introduced into knowledge, besides the <u>data of sense</u>, <u>other elements</u>—elements which legitimated to his own mind his constructive theory of the universe. Accordingly, if we develop his theory of "notions," we arrive at a philosophy which bears a striking resemblance to the rational or spiritual Idealism of to-day, whether that is founded on Kant and Hegel, or has its origin nearer home. In proportion, however, as this side is developed, Berkeley ceases to be liable to the censures which Reid levels at the Cartesian system, and becomes his fellow-combatant against it. In this aspect of his system, we have therefore no right to follow Berkeley at present. And inasmuch as these elements were left undeveloped by Berkeley himself in his influential works; inasmuch as *the necessity of their introduction* was not convincingly reasoned out; and they appear, therefore, rather as unauthorised assumptions — incongruous patches upon the unrepudiated garment of Lockian principles,—we cannot help recognising in Hume the legitimate development of Berkeley's youthful metaphysics. It was natural for Hume to ignore the new and fragmentary constructive suggestions, and to carry further that negative criticism of Locke, which commended itself so highly to his passionless intellect. He was not concerned with Berkeley's individual philosophy, but he was keenly interested in drawing the ultimate consequences of philosophical principles generally accepted. He found that Berkeley helped him on his way, and he did not forget to acknowledge the debt.

On the whole, it is merely aid and suggestion which Hume derives from Berkeley. In his main positions he attaches himself directly to Locke, and works out his results independently. It is often wonderful to see how little transformation requires to be made in Locke's theory. His sentences are simply placed in another setting, and the theory reappears with an entirely new face upon it.

For the term "idea," which plays so great a part in Locke and Berkeley, Hume substitutes the term "perception," to denote the mental units or "distinct existences"[1] which form his sole assumptions. Perceptions are then divided into two classes, impressions and ideas. "The difference betwixt these consists in the degrees of force and liveliness with which they strike upon the mind. . . . Those perceptions which enter with most force and violence we may name impressions. . . . By ideas I mean the faint images of these in thinking and reasoning."[2] Hume adds a note to say that by the term "impression" he does not mean "to express the manner in which our lively perceptions are produced in the soul, but merely the perceptions themselves." Locke, on the other hand, had generally assumed, in a vague way, that each simple idea carried the theory of its origin with it, and announced itself as the idea, or quality, of a thing. Berkeley had denied this inference in words, and had made an effort to treat the ideas as mere ideas. But in a less naïve way he found the same causal reference implied; he made it matter of explicit inference from the involuntary character of our sense-ideas and from their orderly connection. In itself, however, the involuntariness of sense-ideas would

[1] Treatise of Human Nature (Green's edition), i. 559.
[2] Ibid., i. 311.

be only one feeling more, and would not ground any causal judgment, except to one who assumed the relation of causality as known and valid. Not being prepared for such an assumption at the outset, Hume cuts short the question of the cause of our impressions as a transcendent inquiry, which does not arise so long as we are content, in the genuine spirit of "the experimental method," simply to investigate the facts before us—"the perceptions themselves." "To form the idea of an object, and to form an idea simply, is the same thing; the reference of the idea to an object being an extraneous denomination, of which in itself it bears no mark or character."[1] Here, then, at last we have the law laid down on the subject without ambiguity.

At other times, it is true, when he is not thinking of his own analysis of causation, Hume involuntarily assumes some cause of our "impressions of sensation," only insisting that the nature of the cause must inevitably remain obscure.[2] "By what argument can it be proved," he asks in the 'Inquiry,' arguing more popularly and polemically with Locke and common-sense in view, "that the perceptions of the mind must be caused by external objects entirely different

[1] Treatise, i. 327.     [2] Cf. ibid., i. 383.

from them, though resembling them (if that be possible), and could not arise either from the energy of the mind itself, or from the suggestion of some invisible and unknown spirit, or from some other cause still more unknown to us? . . . Here experience is and must be entirely silent. The mind has never anything present to it but the perceptions, and cannot possibly reach the experience of their connection with objects. The supposition of such a connection is therefore without any foundation in reasoning."[1] As for Berkeley's hypothesis, we may read Hume's answer from the remarks which he makes in a different connection upon the "theory of the universal energy and operation of the Supreme Being." "It is too bold," he says, "ever to carry conviction with it to a man sufficiently apprised of the weakness of human reason. Though the chain of arguments which conduct to it were ever so logical, there must arise a strong suspicion, if not an absolute assurance, that it has carried us quite beyond the reach of our faculties, when it leads to conclusions so extraordinary and so remote from common life and experience. We are got into fairyland long ere we have reached the last steps of our

[1] Inquiry, section 12.

theory; and there we have no reason to trust our common methods of argument. . . . Our line is too short to fathom such immense abysses."[1] In other words, he returns to the conclusion alone consonant with his own philosophy: The reference of an idea to an object is an extraneous denomination; the mind, having never anything present to it but the perceptions, cannot possibly reach the experience of their connection with objects. The expectation of causal connection being furthermore, in the strictest sense, a growth of experience, we have no right to apply it transcendently, as Kant would have said—that is, to matters that lie entirely out of the sphere of experience. The real background of the ideas or perceptions, whether material as with Locke, or theological as with Berkeley, is simply wiped out by Hume from his theory.

It follows from the definition of impressions and ideas, that we can have ideas only when we have previously had the relative impressions; for ideas are the faint images of impressions. Where the opportunity of having the impressions is absent, as in the case of one born blind, there we find that the corresponding ideas—the ideas of sight—are likewise absent. Impressions, then,

[1] Inquiry, section 7.

are the ultimate standard of reality; and this furnishes Hume with what Reid humorously calls his "articles of inquisition." " It must be some one impression which gives rise to every real idea. . . . When we entertain any suspicion that a philosophical term is employed without any meaning or idea (as is but too frequent), we need but inquire *from what impression is that supposed idea derived?* . . . Does it arise from an impression of sensation or of reflection? Point it out distinctly to us, that we may know its nature and qualities. But if you cannot point out *any such impression*, you may be certain you are mistaken when you imagine you have *any such idea*."[1] "Without being allowed to offer anything in arrest of judgment," says Reid, "the prisoner is sentenced to pass out of existence, and to be, in all time to come, an empty unmeaning sound or the ghost of a departed entity."[2] In adopting this touchstone, Hume merely emphasises the avowed principles of Locke; but from its announcement in this explicit fashion, it is easy to see that we may expect a far more vigorous sifting of the contents of the mind than we found in either Locke

---

[1] Treatise, i. 533 and 369. Inquiry, section 2; cf. also section 7.
[2] Works, p. 144.

or Berkeley. And one result will be that those conceptions for which no impression is forthcoming—which are different from impressions, and which never existed as impressions—will have to be explained as illusions. It will have to be shown how they would naturally arise, even in the absence of any corresponding reality.

When we pass from the particular perceptions as so many distinct existences, to their combinations and conjunctions, we find Hume still following closely in the footsteps of Locke and Berkeley. The line of thought which he pursues is contained in the account of substance and cause given by his predecessors. "We come," says Locke, "to have the ideas of particular sorts of substances by collecting such combinations of simple ideas as are, by experience and observation of men's senses, taken notice of to exist together. . . . [Such] simple ideas . . . carry with them in their own nature no visible necessary connection or inconsistency with any other simple ideas."[1] Of the closely related idea of cause, he says: "We cannot with certainty affirm that no man can be nourished by wood or stones, that all men will be poisoned by hemlock. . . . We cannot tell what effects [bodies] will produce; nor

[1] Essay, ii. 23, 3; and iv. 3, 10.

when we see those effects can we so much as guess, much less know, their manner of production. . . . The things that, as far as our observation reaches, we constantly find to proceed regularly, we may conclude to act by a law set them, but yet by a law that we know not. . . . We cannot but ascribe them to the arbitrary will and good pleasure of the wise Architect."[1] This is the very conception of the order of nature which Berkeley pressed home. There is no word oftener in his mouth than "arbitrary," to designate the connections we discover between the ideas of sense. The judgments we make in such matters, he declares (to quote only a single passage), " do not arise from any essential or necessary, but only *a customary tie* which has been observed betwixt [the ideas]."[2] Berkeley, as we know, after emptying sense-phenomena altogether of real causality, refunded all efficient power or agency into spiritual Will. When contemplated, therefore, from the objective side, the "customary tie" between sense-ideas becomes, for him as for Locke, "the arbitrary imposition of Providence."[3] The laws of nature,

[1] Essay, iv. 6, 15; iv. 3, 26-28. A great number of passages to the same effect will be found collected in an article by Dr Hutchison Stirling, Mind, ix. pp. 534-536.
[2] New Theory of Vision, section 62.
[3] Alciphron, Fourth Dialogue, section 10.

or the so-called causal relations of ideas to each other, become " the set rules or established methods wherein the Mind we depend on excites in us the ideas of sense."[1] But it may fairly be argued that this is a point to which experience, conceived as Locke and Berkeley conceived it, cannot testify. Experience, as we know it, is, according to Berkeley, a series of independent states, ideas, or perceptions, which, by the non-rational force of custom, we come in course of time to associate with one another in various ways. Now, *unless we start with the presupposition of the rationality of the universe*, we are not justified in assuming that this custom-bred association on our part corresponds to the modes of operation of an objective Will which we were intended to learn. Berkeley certainly makes this tacit presupposition, or takes the rationality of the universe as implied in his own conscious existence. And as he has already satisfied himself, arguing from the same datum, that the only possible cause of our sense-ideas is Spirit, so here the subjective view-point—customary association—is never severed by him from the objective view-point of a divine sense-symbolism. But Hume, having already wiped out the spiritual cause or originator of our perceptions, naturally

[1] Principles, section 30.

declines to call in such an explanation of the arbitrary connections which the perceptions exhibit. In his character as consistent sceptic, he is not prepared to yield Berkeley his implied postulate of the rationality of existence, and is even prepared, as we shall see, to derationalise the citadel of Self, which forms Berkeley's basis of operation. Accordingly, in the present case, he has merely to point out that we are gratuitously going beyond our record, and unnecessarily giving a double explanation of the same fact. The fact of the <u>coherence of perceptions</u>—or, more strictly, the <u>association of certain impressions with certain ideas</u>—is sufficiently explained, so far as we are concerned, by the operation of <u>custom</u>. Why should we suppose that any other explanation is required?

Hume, therefore, stereotyped Berkeley's view of the arbitrariness of natural connections in his famous distinction between <u>relations of ideas</u> and <u>matters of fact</u>. The quotations I have given might be multiplied tenfold; but they are enough to prove that, to an attentive reader of Locke and Berkeley, Hume's celebrated account of <u>causality</u> really contains nothing new. It is simply detached from all that accompanies it and modifies its force in Berkeley. It is put in the foreground, and is made to engross the reader's attention; and finally, it is applied to dissolve every permanent reality completely away. But the theory itself is perfectly inevitable, if we start with relationless units of impression. Each unit exists on its own account, and is independent of all the rest. "Every effect," as Hume says, "is a distinct event from its cause. It could not, therefore, be discovered in the cause.... There is nothing in any object, considered in itself, which can afford us a reason for drawing a conclusion beyond it."[1] We have started, in other words, with indifferent side-by-sideness or indifferent sequence; and indifferent sequence it will remain till the end of the chapter. "All events," as Hume puts it, "seem entirely loose and separate. One event follows another, but we never can observe any tie between them. They seem *conjoined*, but never *connected*."[2]

It is Hume's merit to have made this sensational atomism as plain as it was possible to make it. True, he does not strip his impressions quite bare of relations. Referring only to his own list, we find him taking four "relations of ideas" for granted, as intuitively perceived—viz., resem-

[1] Inquiry, section 4; and Treatise, i. 436.
[2] Inquiry, section 7.

blance, contrariety, arithmetical relations, and degrees of quality.¹ He is, of course, not entitled to these on his own principles; but the total absence of relations would evidently prevent his getting under way at all. We may, therefore, merely note the assumptions. But Hume further illegitimately adds to them time and space. That, at least, is the result of his shuffling account of these ideas. He would apparently have us believe that he has shown the idea of extension to be identical with impressions of colour. But he has before treated it as derivable from " the impressions of coloured points *disposed in a certain manner.*" ² And of time he says similarly that the idea " is not derived from a particular impression, but arises altogether from the manner in which impressions appear to the mind, without making one of the number." ³ And he concludes in regard to both: " The ideas of space and time are therefore no separate or distinct ideas, but merely those of the manner or order in which objects exist." ⁴ These passages are of great importance, in view of what was afterwards con-

---

¹ Treatise, i. 373.
² Ibid., i. 341. Cf. Green's criticism in the Introduction, p. 201.
³ Treatise, i. 343.      ⁴ Ibid., i. 346.

tended both by Kant and Reid. They exhibit Hume himself obliged to call in more than unrelated particulars—obliged to admit ideas for which no corresponding impression can be shown. Time and space are, by his own showing, two different manners in which perceptions are disposed, and in virtue of which they necessarily lose their character of isolated particulars. Every moment of time, every point of space, refers itself infinitely to other moments or points. We may go further, and make the statement quite general. So far is it from being true, as Hume says, that there is nothing in any object, considered in itself, which can afford us a reason for drawing a conclusion beyond it, that the exact contrary might be formulated and defended. The mind is incapable of considering any object in itself; every object carries us necessarily beyond itself, and forces us to recognise its connection with other objects. As regards causality, it is surely time that we emancipated ourselves from the philosophic superstition that connection is simply collocation or succession. As an event, the effect may be regarded as, in a sense, "distinct from its cause." But to treat it merely as an event is to look only at its particularity—to take it as an empty characterless point. No effect, however, is merely an event; every event has a character, is such-and-such an event. It is at its such-and-suchness, at its character—in other words, at the universal in it—that we have to look. As soon as we do so, we see that it is the same universal, present in both cause and effect, which locks them together into a single fact. So far from its being true that " we are never able to discover any quality which binds the effect to the cause," it is precisely the *same* fact which is present in the two particulars and reduces them to intelligibility. Causes and effects are not merely repeated conjunctions of loose and separate events; it would be truer to say, as science itself now says, that the effect *is* the cause.

But we must follow Hume a little further, in order to gain a complete view of the consequences to which he leads us. His whole system was already contained, as has been remarked, in the initial assumption of particular perceptions inherited by him from Locke and Berkeley. Hume's whole task was, not to prove that things *are* abstract or unrelated particulars, but, assuming them to be such, to show how *the illusion* of real connection between mutually indifferent units might arise. This is the meaning and scope of his analysis of the idea of causality. "Necessity," he concludes, "is something that exists in the mind, not in the objects. . . . The idea arises from the repetition of their union; the repetition neither discovers nor causes anything in the objects, but has an influence only on the mind by that customary transition it produces."[1] And he does not stop short at the confines of the material world, as Berkeley had done; he extends his analysis with rigorous consistency to the action of Spirit or Will. "So far from perceiving the connection betwixt an act of volition and a motion of the body, 'tis allowed that no effect is more inexplicable from the powers and essence of thought and matter. Nor is the empire of the will over the mind more intelligible. The effect is there distinguishable and separable from the cause, and could not be foreseen without the experience of their constant conjunction."[2] Here, as elsewhere, it is custom which produces a vivid imaginative transition; and this, again, is identical with Belief.

This custom-bred transition being established as the sole origin of the connections commonly supposed to exist between matters of fact, it is next applied to explain the illusion of identity in objects—that is, the illusion of a permanent material

[1] Treatise, i. 461.  [2] Ibid., p. 455.

world, or, as Hume puts it, of a continued and distinct existence of our perceptions. The notion of the identity of objects is due, he maintains, to "the smooth and uninterrupted progress of the imagination" along a series of closely resembling perceptions. "The imagination, when set into any train of thinking, is apt to continue, even when its object fails it, and, like a galley put in motion by the oars, carries on its course without any new impulse."[1] In this way, it first converts resemblance into numerical identity, and then, being uneasy on account of the interruptions which the existence of this identical object suffers during the intervals of non-perception, it completes its constructive work by the fiction of a continued existence during these uncomfortable gaps. This is the point at which the *vulgar* stand. But here the imagination is brought to book by reason. Reason points out the absurdity of attributing independent existence to perceptions: an unperceived perception is a contradiction in terms. Hence arises the *philosophical* hypothesis of a "double existence of perceptions and objects: which pleases our reason in allowing that our dependent perceptions are interrupted and different; and at the same time is agreeable

[1] Treatise, i. 487.

to the imagination, in attributing a continued existence to something else, which we call objects."[1] The philosophical system, therefore, has nothing in the facts to recommend it. It is only a patch upon the errors of the imagination, and but for these errors would never have been devised. As Hume says, it derives all its authority from the vulgar system. The logical consequence to which philosophical reflection leads, is that our perceptions have no more a continued than an independent existence. If we resist the irrational promptings of the imagination at the outset, we shall then rest content with our perceptions as they are. "Since all our perceptions are different from each other, and from everything else in the universe, they are also distinct and separable, and may be considered separately existent, and may exist separately, and have no need of anything else to support their existence."[2]

But if this is really so, why should we continue to treat them as the perceptions of a Self? Why should we speak as if they required a self or mind for their subsistence? This is the one notion still awaiting dissolution at Hume's hands; and at the end of the first volume of the 'Treatise,'

[1] Treatise, i. 502.    [2] Ibid., i. 518. Cf. also i. 495.

he brings his old battery to bear upon it. "From what impression could this idea be derived? . . . If any impression gives rise to the idea of self, that impression must continue invariably the same through the whole course of our lives; since self is supposed to exist after that manner. But there is no impression constant and invariable. Pain and pleasure, grief and joy, passions and sensations, succeed each other, and never all exist at the same time. It cannot, therefore, be from any of these impressions, or from any other, that the idea of self is derived; and, consequently, *there is no such idea.*"[1] The illusion arises from the same propensity of the imagination which has been noted in the case of material things. It proceeds "entirely from the smooth and uninterrupted progress of the thought along a train of connected ideas." The principles of association, more particularly those of <u>resemblance</u> and <u>causation</u>, "convey the imagination . . . from one link to another;" and from this, the passage is easy to "some fiction or imaginary principle of union."[2]

It is perhaps noteworthy that this analysis of the <u>Self</u> is introduced at the end of the whole discussion, and that in Hume's easier version of

[1] Treatise, i. 533.   [2] Ibid., i. 541-543.

his doctrine, in the 'Inquiry,' it is dropped altogether. In resolving the world of things into intermittent mind-dependent perceptions, and in resolving causation into frequently observed contiguity and the mental habit thence arising, it was almost necessary to suppose a mind present to undertake these manifold functions. It might have been embarrassing, at that stage, to have been obliged to reflect that the Self too, like the other principles of real connection, is a fiction. And this is not the only instance in which Hume has chosen his order of discussion most adroitly for his own purposes. But here even Hume's ingenuity and passion for consistency are not enough to carry his thesis through. For what do we mean by saying that the perceptions which constitute the mind naturally introduce each other? We mean, according to Hume himself, that memory, in reviewing the " system of different perceptions or different existences," to which we erroneously ascribe an identity, is constantly led on by the associative tendency from one member of the system to another. Association does its work, therefore, for the reviewing eye of memory; so that memory, as Hume truly says, is the real source of personal identity.[1] But

[1] Treatise, i. 542.

what is this memory but a second Ego, raising its head resistlessly behind the first which we discarded? Or what is the imagination, which plays so great a part in the Humian system, but the same hardly veiled reintroduction of the Ego? "Identity," it is said, "is nothing really belonging to the different perceptions, and uniting them together; but is merely a quality, which we attribute to them, *because of the union of their ideas in the imagination, when we reflect upon them.*"[1] They *are* united, then, somewhere, in spite of all disclaimers; and whether the principle of union be called Memory, or Imagination, or Self, is of comparatively little account.

It has thus been shown incidentally that even Hume is not perfectly faithful to his philosophical principles. The Ego—the central principle of connection—is found to resist his efforts. Time and Space are also principles of connection which he first tries to ignore or explain away, and then unwarrantably assumes. The four relations of ideas which he assumes as intuitively perceived, are likewise inconsistent additions to a theory which professes to found on pure particulars. But such inconsequences, it must be repeated, were necessary, if the theory was to come to

[1] Treatise, i. 540.

speech at all. And we are less concerned with Hume's inconsequences than with the drift of his whole argument—the goal which, it must be allowed, he did his best to reach, and which he points out with singular clearness to be the inevitable implication of the principles which he inherited, and which he assumes throughout.

In the short Appendix which he added to the third volume of the 'Treatise' in 1740, Hume expressly connects himself with the preceding development of philosophy. "Philosophers begin to be reconciled," he says, "to the principle that we have no idea of external substance, distinct from the ideas of particular qualities. This must pave the way for a like principle with regard to the mind, that we have no notion of it distinct from the particular perceptions."[1] This consummation has been attained, he means to say, in his own philosophy. He claims, in his own admirable phrase, to have "loosened all our particular perceptions." Two principles, as he points out, constitute the Alpha and the Omega of his philosophy. The first is, that "perceptions are distinct existences;" and the second is, that "the mind never perceives any real connection among distinct existences." The second is the immedi-

[1] Treatise, i. 559.

ate consequence of the first; and between the two lies the *rationale* of Hume's whole industry. If it be true that all our perceptions are distinct, or, as we have seen him put it in another passage, "different from each other and from everything else in the universe," then the possibility of real connection is excluded *ab initio;* it would contradict our own definition. The units are indifferent, and they merely remain so; they are so many distinct mental events—and "all events," Hume tells us, "are entirely loose and separate." There remains only the plausible explanation of the way in which the illusion of connection, in its different forms, grows upon us. Here Hume is free to confess that he is not thoroughly satisfied with his own constructive theory, and he does so in a remarkable passage of this Appendix. It is in connection with personal identity that the difficulty chiefly comes home to him. Others may solve the difficulty, he says, and produce a system more satisfactory to reason; but for himself he pleads "the privilege of a sceptic." The inability which he here acknowledges to reconstruct without some principle of real connection, does not, however, lead him to reconsider the twin principles or assumptions on which his philosophy depends. It is not in his power, he says, to renounce either of them. This renunciation was left for Reid and Kant; and Hume's system remains, therefore, the apotheosis, or, we might better say, the self-refutation of the doctrine of the abstract particular.

Philosophy could go no further without a reconsideration of this fundamental dogma of the Lockian philosophy. This was clearly seen both by Reid and Kant. "Ideas," says Reid, "were first introduced into philosophy in the humble character of images or representatives of things; and in this character they seemed not only to be inoffensive, but to serve admirably well for explaining the operations of the human understanding. But since men began to reason clearly and distinctly about them, they have, by degrees, supplanted their constituents, and undermined the existence of everything but themselves.... These ideas are as free and independent as the birds of the air.... Yet, after all, these self-existent and independent ideas look pitifully naked and destitute, when left thus alone in the universe, set adrift without a rag to cover their nakedness."[1] Reid shares with Kant the merit of taking Hume always in his true charac-

[1] Works, p. 109.

ter as a sceptic, and treating his system strictly as a *reductio ad impossibile* of accepted philosophical principles. "I acknowledge," he says, in the Dedication of his first work, "that I never thought of calling in question the principles commonly received with regard to the human understanding, until the 'Treatise of Human Nature' was published in the year 1739. The ingenious author of that treatise upon the principles of Locke—who was no sceptic—hath built a system of scepticism which leaves no ground to believe any one thing rather than its contrary. His reasoning appeared to me to be just; there was therefore a necessity to call in question the principles upon which it was founded, or to admit the conclusion."[1] That the conclusion *could* be admitted by sober men as a reasonable, credible, or even plausible theory of the facts, does not seem to have occurred to him. He would simply have stared, if he had been told that generations of English thinkers would take Hume *au grand sérieux*, and adopt his speculations as a constructive theory of knowledge. In this, Reid shows a far truer instinct than is shown, for example, in Professor Huxley's able and brilliant, but extremely unsatisfactory,

[1] Works, p. 95.

study of the great sceptic. His scepticism disappears altogether in Professor Huxley's account, and he is made the pioneer of scientific method. This is a strange distinction for the man who sums up his position by saying that "if we believe that fire warms, or water refreshes, 'tis only because it costs us too much pains to think otherwise."[1]

In treating Hume as such a *reductio*, it is not, of course, maintained that he saw, so to speak, beyond himself. No man is two personalities in this way. Nor are we to suppose that Hume saw the fallacy or insufficiency of the principles he adopted from Locke, and that he therefore, of deliberate purpose, set about a laborious refutation of them by reducing them to their ultimate consequences. His philosophy is not a prolonged and conscious irony of this description. On the contrary, there is no reason to doubt that he accepted in perfect good faith the fundamental positions from which he argued. He saw no others equally plausible; and when he had given free scope to his logical acuteness, he stranded himself equally with his masters on the consequences he arrived at. As a philosopher, he had no city of refuge to which he

[1] Treatise, i. 549.

could flee from the results of his own reasoning, though, as a man of the world, he was not without resource. To begin again at the beginning, and re-examine his premisses, as Reid called upon him to do, might have "cost him too much pains," after he had already worked out his metaphysical vein in three large volumes. But (however much we may be willing, as agnostics, to narrow our horizon), we are surely precluded by Hume's own language, not to speak of his manner, from imagining, as Professor Huxley seems to suppose, that, on reviewing his conclusions as a whole, he regarded them as a tenable theory of the facts. No doubt Hume thought, especially as his life wore on, that an important indirect advantage was to be gained from his speculations in the blow they administered to the old giant Superstition; and it may readily be admitted that this was a main motive with him in the reproduction or new version of his philosophy which he gave in the 'Inquiry,' and from which, it should be remarked, Professor Huxley mainly quotes. But in his youthful work his philosophical ardour was purer; he was sustained there by an unselfish intellectual enthusiasm, which aimed at thoroughness and completeness for their own sakes. And at the end of his comprehensive survey, he found that his results, *if taken seriously*, were anything but consolatory. "A malady to be cured," "clouds to be dispelled," "philosophical melancholy and delirium"—these are some of the names he applies to his speculations. "This sceptical doubt," he says, "is a malady which can never be radically cured; it always increases, the further we carry our reflections. Carelessness and inattention alone can afford us any remedy. . . . I dine, I play a game of backgammon, I converse and am merry with my friends; and when, after three or four hours' amusement, I would return to these speculations, they appear so cold, and strained, and ridiculous, that I cannot find in my heart to enter into them any further."[1] Is this the language of one who puts forward his system as a theory to be believed and acted upon, seriously lived up to, as Professor Huxley would have us believe? A philosophy which must be abandoned in order to perform the most ordinary offices of life can hardly be the satisfactory foundation of science and conduct which some have professed to find it.

In refusing to look upon Hume's system as a substantive or serious account of the nature of things, we are simply taking him at his own

[1] Treatise, i. 501, 548.

valuation. Universal scepticism is, indeed, a malady which cannot be cured. But it is equally a position in which reason finds it impossible for a moment to rest. Universal scepticism would be justified only on the supposition that the world is *absolutely* incapable of being rationalised—incapable, that is to say, in any degree or to any, however small an extent. But the confidence, or, if we like to call it so, the faith of reason in itself is indestructible and inexhaustible; and faith in itself means faith also in the ultimate rationality of the universe. Scepticism, therefore, can never, as Kant puts it, be a permanent state for human reason. It is the transition from one constructive system to another. Systems will never fail, as long as man retains at once his reason and his finitude. Scepticism is the bridge by which we pass from one system, or family of systems, found wanting, to another age with its fuller grasp of truth.

# LECTURE III.

### THOMAS REID: SENSATION AND PERCEPTION.

IN the two preceding lectures, we have traced in some detail the development of what Reid calls the ideal scepticism. We have now to consider the main drift of Reid's answer to Hume. Quotations have already abundantly shown that Reid had a perfectly clear consciousness of Hume's relation to his philosophical progenitors. He explicitly recognised the necessity of combating the 'Treatise of Human Nature' by striking at its root-assumptions. As Hume's conclusions could not be seriously proposed for acceptance, the only alternative remaining was to attack the πρῶτον ψεῦδος of the theory—the assumption, namely, that experience yields as its ultimate data such self-subsistent, "loose," or relationless units of sensation as Hume begins and ends with. It had to be shown that, so far from being the ultimate elements of knowledge, such ideas or perceptions, "entirely loosened," are not really elements at all, in the sense of being themselves knowable; and that they cannot, therefore, be a possible substructure for the subsequent growth of fictitious relations. Whatever view might ultimately be taken of the function of sense in knowledge, it had to be shown that by themselves such sensational units, instead of being the ultimately real, are only abstractions of the mind. This could evidently be done only by a renewed and more careful analysis of the percipient act; and it was simply such an analysis that Reid and Kant alike undertook. The difficulties of the Lockian account of perception arose, in the main, from the vagueness and looseness with which it employed the term sensation. Sensation was supposed by Locke himself to *give* most of the relations by which we construe the world. The fact that ideas of sensation are often changed by the judgment; or, in more modern phraseology, that the greater part of our adult perception is really acquired perception—that is to say, a mass of judgments grown automatic through habit—seems only to have dawned on him as an afterthought, due to Mr Molyneux, the "thinking gentleman" of Dublin.[1]

[1] See Essay, ii. 9, 8.

In Berkeley and Hume, as the term sensation was progressively defined with a nearer approach to accuracy, the relations which Locke had vaguely included under the term were gradually found to be separable from sensation. They were discovered to be something over and above sensation proper—something, in Hume's phrase, "belonging to the mind." They might be set down either as due to its spontaneous action about its ideas or as generated in it by the flow of the ideas; but in either case they were distinguished from the sense-ideas or the original data themselves. In Reid this process of definition is carried further.

But here at the outset a few words of explanation may be advisable. Scottish philosophy is frequently supposed to be nothing more than an unanalysed and somewhat gross assertion of the dual existence of mind and matter, and the immediate presence of the one to the other. And it is true that if we turn over the pages of the Scottish philosophers, we find what seems a disproportionate amount of talk about the theory of Representative Perception, and about the doctrine of Natural Realism which they oppose to it. This is not, for us, the most vital point from which to attack the general philosophical question. Nevertheless, the instinct of Reid and his followers did not lead them very far astray. For the theory of Representative Perception implies what I have called the two-substance doctrine; and, conversely, if mind and matter are conceived as two self-subsistent substances, essentially distinct the one from the other, the intercourse between the two is of necessity conceived mechanically. The process of knowledge is supposed ultimately to rest upon the repeated momentary contact of the two substances. Each such contact or impact makes its mark upon the mind in the shape of what is called an impression. The detached impressions of the Humian theory are therefore directly connected with the doctrine of two alien substances and the theory of Representative Perception; and accordingly, in attacking Representative Perception, the Scottish philosophers are contributing to the refutation of the fallacies with which it is bound up. I am ready to admit that, in their zeal against a subjective idealism, they have often over-stated their case, and maintained the independence of the material world in terms which imply the old two-substance doctrine. But the Natural Dualism of the school, as it is sometimes called, certainly does not in itself involve this doctrine. On the contrary, by maintaining a theory of Immediate Perception, Scottish philosophy destroys the foreignness of matter to mind, and thus implicitly removes the only foundation of a real dualism. But to approach Scottish philosophy from this side would be to begin at the end rather than at the beginning. We shall best see the importance of Reid's work, and its relation to the work of Kant and German philosophy, by concentrating our attention upon his analysis of Sensation and Perception. Reid's theory here is so admirable, and has been, comparatively speaking, so little attended to, that I will take the liberty of stating it in some detail. We may begin by following Reid for a little in his own method of attacking the question, and then proceed to gather up the results in our own way.

The 'Inquiry'[1] is confined to the five external senses; and Reid begins with the simplest and least intellectual of these—with Smell and Taste—by way of working gradually towards the more

[1] The full title of the book is 'An Inquiry into the Human Mind on the Principles of Common Sense.' It was published in 1764. The 'Essays on the Intellectual Powers of Man' (1785) and the 'Essays on the Active Powers of the Human Mind' (1788) contain a fuller and more systematic account of Reid's philosophy; but in some respects there is more freshness about the earlier work. In what follows, quotations are made indifferently from the 'Inquiry' and the 'Essays.'

complex phenomena of the primary qualities which form the heart of the problem. He joins issue, however, with the ideal system on the very threshold of his investigation. That system started, as we have seen, from un<u>referred</u> perceptions, ideas pure and simple. To Hume's supposed knowledge of "the perceptions themselves," Reid applies the scholastic term <u>Simple Apprehension</u>; and he takes up position at once, by denying that the process of perception is truly described as beginning thus. We do not start, he insists, with ideas, but with <u>judgments.</u> So far from being the primitive act of mind, <u>Simple Apprehension,</u> or the knowledge of sensations *per se*, is a species of abstract contemplation only attainable at a later stage "by resolving and analysing a natural and original judgment." "Apprehension accompanied with belief and knowledge must go before simple apprehension." In other words, we do not have sensations first, and refer them afterwards to a subject and an object; our first having of a sensation is at the same time the knowledge of it as objective and the knowledge of it as mine. Locke's definition of knowledge, therefore, as consisting in a perception of the agreement or disagreement of ideas, is entirely false. We are never restricted to our own ideas; at the very first step we pass beyond our sensations into a real and permanent world on which they depend, and of which they are merely the signs. "It is not," says Reid, "by first having the notions of mind and sensation, and then comparing them together, that we perceive the one to have the relation of a subject or substratum, and the other that of an act or operation; on the contrary, one of the related things—to wit, sensation—suggests to us both the correlate and the relation."[1]

The word *suggestion* is an important one in Reid's philosophy. Reid borrows the word from Berkeley, but he gives it a different application. Berkeley's "suggestions" were the teachings of experience as to the interconnections of sense-phenomena. Reid applies the term especially to denote those "natural suggestions," as he calls them, or "judgments of nature," which are implied in the existence of phenomena at all—relations, in other words, which are necessary to the constitution of experience, yet which cannot be said to be given in impressions or sensations as such, but only to be given *along with* the data of sense proper. The first of these natural suggestions or judgments, as was to be expected, is the

[1] Works, pp. 106-111.

reference of sensations to an Ego or permanent subject. "Thought must have a subject, and be the act of some thinking being. . . . Our sensations and thoughts suggest the notion of a mind, and the belief of its existence, and its relation to our thoughts." This particular notion and belief Berkeley had also held, but without resting it on such broad grounds as those now put forward by Reid. Sensation, according to Reid, suggests the notion and belief; or on the occasion of sensation, we may say, such a judgment is necessarily "suggested by our constitution." "By what principles of logic we make these inferences it is impossible to show." Indeed, we do not make them by any explicit process of reasoning over which logic could claim control; as "first principles," they fall not within the province of reasoning, but of common-sense. Nor is it possible to show how our sensations can give us the notions; all that can be said is what has been said already, that "they are judgments of nature—judgments not got by comparing ideas and perceiving agreements and disagreements, but immediately inspired by our constitution."[1]

This is not the place to enter into a general enumeration and vindication of these first princi-

[1] Works, p. 110.

ples or natural judgments. Those only concern us at present which are necessary for the understanding of Reid's account of Sensation and Perception. A second judgment which every sensation carries with it, so far as it is a possible constituent of knowledge, is that of Existence. Hume, indeed, in a section of his 'Treatise,' had attempted to explain away the involved judgment as nothing beyond the perceptions themselves; but Reid wisely treats this as an insufficient or disingenuous analysis. According to a third of these natural principles, "a beginning of existence, or any change in nature, suggests to us the notion of a cause;" and this judgment also is involved in the perceptive process from the beginning. Any sensation recognised as existing and as beginning to exist is a change in nature which calls for the application of the principle. Experience presently teaches us that the sensation of smell (with which Reid starts) is connected, let us say, with the presence of a rose which our other senses reveal to us. Hence we conclude that there is a quality or virtue in the rose which we call its smell. Not that even the vulgar, Reid continues, imagine "the smell in the rose to be something like to the sensation of smelling;" they are unjustly charged with this absurdity by philosophers, who palm off their paradoxes as profound discoveries. In point of fact, the smell of a rose signifies two things, which only the philosophers show any disposition to confound. "First, a sensation, which can have no existence but when it is perceived, and can only be in a sentient being or mind; secondly, it signifies some power, quality, or virtue in the rose, or in effluvia proceeding from it, which hath a permanent existence, independent of the mind, and which, by the constitution of nature, produces the sensation in us. By the original constitution of our nature, we are both led to believe that there is a permanent cause of the sensation, and prompted to seek after it; and experience determines us to place it in the rose."[1]

But in this, Reid evidently anticipates his own account of the data of the other senses, and, in particular, his account of the natural judgments which accompany the senses of sight and touch. Meanwhile, in dealing with the so-called secondary qualities, he contents himself with pointing out the ambiguity which attaches to the names of all smells, tastes, sounds, as well as heat and cold, inasmuch as there is but one word to cover both the sensations themselves and "the exter-

[1] Works, p. 114.

nal qualities which are indicated by them." He adds, however, that, most properly and commonly, the name is applied to the thing indicated by the sensation. For it is only in certain cases, where sensations "are so quick and lively as to give us a great deal either of pleasure or of uneasiness," that "we are compelled to attend to the sensation itself, and to make it an object of thought and discourse." In such cases (as, for example, in "the various kinds of pain, sickness, and the sensations of hunger and other appetites"), we give a name which signifies nothing but the sensation itself, and about which, therefore, there can be no confusion. In the majority of cases, however, the sensation is not interesting enough in itself to be made an object of thought, and so we pass at once beyond it to the reality which it reveals. "Our constitution," says Reid, "leads us to consider it as a *sign* of something external which hath a constant conjunction with it."[1]

The distinction thus drawn between the sensation and its objective cause becomes of fundamental importance when we pass to the primary qualities. For in their case we have, according to Reid, not only the belief or knowledge of *some* power, quality, or virtue in the object, which,

[1] Works, p. 114.

itself permanent and independent of the mind, produces the sensation in us: we have a perfectly distinct conception of what the cause is. In other words, we have an immediate perception of a certain quality of matter, which has to be carefully distinguished from the sensation, on occasion of which this perception takes place. The risk of confounding the two is, however, greatly increased in the new set of cases. When we come to the sense of Touch, for example, we find that, by its means, we perceive not one quality only but many, and these of different kinds. The chief of them, according to Reid, are heat and cold, hardness and softness, roughness and smoothness, figure, solidity, motion, and extension. We may leave heat and cold aside here, as ranking with secondary qualities; and, of the others, we may select hardness for consideration in the meantime. There is no doubt a sensation, Reid begins, by which we perceive a body to be hard or soft. This is seen when contact is so violent as to cause pain; our attention is then at once turned to the subjective feeling. But by pressing the hand moderately against the table, and attending to the feeling which ensues, while abstracting as much as possible from all thought of the table and its qualities, we may also, he says, make the *sensation* of hardness a distinct object of reflection—though with difficulty. Apart, however, from such a reflective effort, the sensation "is never attended to, but passes through the mind instantaneously, and serves only to introduce that quality in bodies, which, by a law of our constitution, it suggests."[1] We are so accustomed to use the sensation merely as a sign, that it has no name in any language. This must not blind us, however, to the distinction which exists between the sensation and the percept. The sensation we have when touching a hard body, and the perceived hardness of the body, so far from being identical, have not even the slightest resemblance. Upon accurate reflection, they appear, says Reid, "not only to be different things, but as unlike as pain is to the point of a sword."[2]

Now we have "as clear and distinct a conception" of hardness as of anything whatsoever. Accordingly it is a quality of quite a different order from those secondary qualities which we only know as the causes of certain sensations. Though Berkeley, following out the received doctrine of ideas, discarded the distinction between the primary and the secondary qualities, "yet after all," says Reid, "there appears to be a real

[1] Works, p. 120.   [2] Ibid., p. 122.

foundation for it in the principles of our nature." Having made this weighty observation, he goes on, with a "similarly," to extend his argument to roughness and smoothness, figure and motion, and what these "do all suppose"—extension. "All these, *by means of certain corresponding sensations of touch, are presented to the mind as real external qualities;* the conception and the belief of them are invariably connected with the corresponding sensations by an original principle of human nature."[1] "When I grasp a ball in my hand, I perceive it at once hard, figured, and extended. The feeling is very simple, and hath not the least resemblance to any quality of body. Yet it suggests to us three primary qualities perfectly distinct from one another, as well as from the sensation which indicates them." In language which is perfectly applicable to the Sensationalists of to-day, he proceeds: "We are commonly told by philosophers that we get the idea of extension by feeling along the extremities of a body, as if there were no manner of difficulty in the matter. I have sought, with great pains I confess, to find out how this idea can be got by feeling; but I have sought in vain. . . . It is true we have feelings of touch, which every moment present exten-

[1] Works, p. 123.

sion to the mind; but how they come to do so is the question."[1] In a separate section he takes some account of the various ways in which such philosophers suppose us to collect the notion of extension from sensations alone,—*e.g.*, the application of an object to a larger or smaller part of the body, the drawing of an object across the hands or face, or the instinctive movements of the limbs. Can this, he asks, give a man any notion of space or motion? "It no doubt gives a new feeling; but how it should convey a notion of space or motion to one who had none before, I cannot conceive. . . . Such a motion may give a certain succession of feelings, as the colic may do, but no feelings nor any combination of feelings can ever resemble space or motion." "What hath imposed upon philosophers," he concludes, "is that the feelings of touch which suggest primary qualities, have no names. . . . They are natural signs, and the mind immediately passes to the thing signified, without making the least reflection upon the sign, or observing that there was any such thing."[2]

Reid cautiously disentangles himself from the historical question whether "the sensations of touch do, from the very first, suggest the same

[1] Works, p. 124.  [2] Ibid., pp. 124, 126.

notions of body and its qualities which they do when we are grown up." "Perhaps," he suggests, "a child in the womb, or for some short period of its existence, is merely a sentient being."[1] But that is really a question which does not concern us. The philosophical point is the complete or generic distinction between Perception and Sensation—between Knowledge and Feeling—which for ever precludes any derivation of the one from the other. On this distinction Reid is prepared to stake the whole question between himself and the ideal scepticism.[2] It is the same issue by which Kant also chooses to abide.

There is just one point in the above analysis which is open to criticism, and that is Reid's assertion that we have, or may have, a knowledge of the sensational signs apart from any perceptive reference to an external object. He makes this statement again, unreservedly, and indeed emphatically, in distinguishing between the material impression and the sensation, both of which are, according to his theory, antecedent conditions of perception. "Nature carries on the first part of the process of perception without our consciousness or concurrence. But we cannot be

[1] Works, p. 130.  [2] See ibid., p. 128.

unconscious of the next step in this process—the sensation of the mind, which always immediately follows the impression made upon the body. It is essential to a sensation to be felt, and it can be nothing more than we feel it to be. If we can only acquire the habit of attending to our sensations, we may know them perfectly."[1] Such sensations would seem to bear a suspicious resemblance to the unreferred ideas which he combats. It is true, as may be proved from other passages, that Reid does not mean to assert the possibility of sensations apart from the reference to a subject; so that, to that extent, he preserves the element of judgment. But he distinctly denies the necessary reference to an object. "Sensation," he says, "taken by itself, implies neither the conception nor belief of any external object. It supposes a sentient being and a certain manner in which that being is affected; but it supposes no more."[2] But if this is so (even in the case of the secondary qualities), then we really begin as subjective idealists, with a fleeting internal world, which we only afterwards refer to an external and permanent one. Reid's statement, therefore, sublates his own position, if it be taken to refer to the original

[1] Works, p. 187.   [2] Ibid., p. 312.

act of perception. But, in all probability, he was thinking of a subsequent act of analysis or abstraction, to which the name "simple apprehension" might be given. "*With some pains and practice,*" he says, "I can form as clear a notion of the other sensations of touch as I have of pain." Evidently what he means here is a certain localised affection of the bodily organism, recognised as such. But this already involves extension and all its consequences. It has all the determinations of the object; it is a percept, and not by any means the original sensational sign of which we are in quest. In the case Reid refers to, all that we do is to abstract from certain relations, in order to concentrate our attention upon others which are normally less prominent. It is misleading, therefore, to speak as if we ever reached, in actual life, the sensations which we postulate as the signs or occasions of our perceptions.

This is borne out by Reid's embarrassment when he comes to treat of the sense of Sight. The optical sensation of the eye *per se* is colour; but we never see colour without seeing it extended. What we see is a coloured expanse of uncertain limits, which we call the field of vision. This is true of the eye at rest, and would be true even of an hypothetical eye which had never moved. So much is recognised by modern psychology, which makes no distinction in principle between the case of impact upon the retina and impact upon the skin or ordinary touch. In both cases, every part of the sensitive surface must possess what is called a "local colouring" or a "local sign" of its own, which yields, on interpretation, the position in space of the object (or relative part of the object) causing the affection. This is the conclusion of the most exact modern psychology, as we find it in Lotze, in Wundt, or in Sully. Our sensations of sight and touch are, in adult life, immediately and automatically localised, or referred to objects in space. But the sensations must carry with them some qualitative difference, in virtue of which the localisation takes place at one point rather than at another. In our conscious life, however, the extensional reference is everywhere present; we are unable to speak or to think without it. And hence we never reach in knowledge what Sully advisedly calls "this unknown original difference."[1] In the case of the local signs of the retinal surface, it is, if possible, more evident than in the similar local signs of the tactual surface, that they are quite incognisable for us,

[1] Outlines of Psychology, p. 119.

save as objectively interpreted in terms of perception. Translated into Reid's language, this means that, in the case of visible figure, the sensational sign which suggests it is not in itself an object of knowledge. This Reid sees very clearly; but he overleaps himself in stating the fact, and, in this one case, denies the presence of any sensational sign at all. "The position of the coloured thing is no sensation; but it is, by the laws of my constitution, presented to the mind along with the colour, *without any additional sensation.*" And again: "There seems to be no sensation that is appropriated to visible figure or whose office it is to suggest it. It seems to be suggested immediately by the material impression upon the organ, of which we are not conscious." [1] Visible figure is once more expressly mentioned in a later section as an exception to the general rule.[2] But enough has been said to show that, in point of unknowableness, all sensations as such stand upon the same footing. On the other hand, such unknowableness being admitted of all, there is no reason for denying, in this particular case, the presence of some local sign — some extra-sensation besides colour—which yields on interpretation the position and visible size of an

[1] Works, pp. 145, 146.   [2] Ibid., p. 187.

object. Visible and tangible extension stand here on precisely the same footing; the sensations must contain some specific indication or hint as to the whereabouts of the object, if our location of the latter is not to be purely arbitrary. From the psychological side, we are bound to regard such an indication as itself a sensation; from the physiological side, we naturally look on the sign as inherent in the organic impression or stimulus, and we speak, in this particular instance, of a *retinal* sign. Both ways of speaking are equally legitimate; the psychological is really simply a translation of the physiological. For every shade of difference in the material facts must have its mental correlate; differences in the stimuli must have corresponding differences in the sensations. It is therefore in deference to physiological results that we assume psychological elements which, in themselves, we cannot be said to know, and which psychology by its method of introspection alone could never have reached.[1]

The essence of Scottish philosophy, as it appears in Reid, is accordingly a vindication of per-

[1] Altogether, the language in which the most accurate psychologists have come to speak of sensation is sufficiently instructive. "Pure sensation," says Wundt (Physiologische

ception, as perception, in contradistinction to the vague sensational idealism, which had ended in the disintegration of knowledge. Sensation is the condition of Perception; but so far from the two terms being interchangeable, sensation, as sensation, does not enter into perception at all. It is significant that the two points on which Reid takes his stand should be (1) the reassertion of the essential difference between the primary and the secondary qualities, or, in other words, the proclamation of the impassable gulf between extension, as a percept, and any feeling or series of feelings; and (2) the assertion that the unit of knowledge is an act of judgment. These are the hinges, it is hardly necessary to add, upon which Kant's philosophy also turns—in the Æsthetic and the Analytic.

As regards the *first* point, it will be remembered that the main drift of the philosophy of Berkeley and Hume was to obliterate the tradi-

Psychologie, ii. 196), "is an abstraction which never occurs in consciousness. None the less, we are forced to assume that our ideas (Vorstellungen) are everywhere formed out of sensations by a psychological synthesis." We might perhaps compare Hamilton's at first sight paradoxical statement (Lectures on Metaphysics, i. 348) : " I do not hesitate to maintain that what we are conscious of is constructed out of what we are not conscious of—that our whole knowledge, in fact, is made up of the unknown and the incognisable."

tional and common-sense distinction between the primary and secondary qualities, which Locke had still maintained. By separating tangible from visible extension, and dwelling almost exclusively on the perception of distance, Berkeley had seemed to resolve space altogether into a series of sensations of locomotive effort. But it gradually becomes apparent that this is really an analysis of space into time—*i.e.*, there is dropped out in the process the distinguishing characteristic of space—the coexistence of points. We have already mentioned Hume's equivocation between impressions of colour and " coloured points" or " coloured points disposed in a certain order." The use of the word point, and still more of the longer phrase, assumes everything. But any number of *minima sensibilia*, or units of sense, remain, as such, discrete and separate—perishing existences. Without time, there is no continuous element in which we can in any wise pass from the one to the other; and without space there is no order of coexistence in which they may be disposed in reference to one another. Time and space, it is true, are nothing to us without the *minima sensibilia* — without their contents—but it is equally true that the *minima sensibilia* cannot exist as such, except as presented in time and space. In virtue of such presentation, they become capable of reference to other contents of time and space, and are thereby recognised as members of a permanent world. It is impossible, therefore, either to eliminate space or to reduce it to simpler elements. And, as we have just seen, the more closely psychologists and physiologists have investigated the problem, the more clearly has this been established. Professor Bain did good service to psychology by insisting on the importance of sensations of movement in the development of our idea of space. But motor sensations *plus* sensations of touch are not enough, it is now admitted, unless the tactual sensations, as depending on the stimulation of distinct nerve-fibres, have each a peculiar local colouring of their own. What is this but to give up the problem, and to end by explaining space by itself? Space, according to Wundt, is the result of a psychical synthesis, which does not admit of being again resolved into its elements. The elements are never known separately; but, so far as our research carries us, they may be taken as sensations of movement or innervation, *plus* sensations of touch, *plus* the local characteristics which attach to the latter. Thus the researches of the physiological psychologists have been useful in pointing out the several elements by the help of which, or on occasion of which, the mind comes to perceive space. But the distinctive element in the synthesis—or, in other words, Space, the synthesis itself—remains after the analysis just where it was. It cannot be explained into anything else; it can only be named. It is a fact not without significance when the editor of 'Mind' (at the close of a very careful article on the respective functions of Psychology and Philosophy) is found laying it down as one of the "points in the philosophical theory of knowledge which, since the time of Kant, may be regarded as placed beyond reasonable question, that we know Space, abstractly, as a 'form' inclusive of sensation, and, actually, as one great *continuum* (percept not concept) within which all sensible objects are ordered."[1]

The fact is stated in Kantian language; and this is no more than justice, seeing that it was in Kant's hands that the distinction between sensation and the form or element which is necessary to its perceptive reality, first acquired world-wide celebrity. Kant made the distinction with a sharpness and a clearness which no one had shown before. But the substantial fact was

[1] Mind, viii. 21.

stated by Reid, though he lacked the art to make his discoveries as impressive and prominent as they became in the hands of his German contemporary. "Space," he says, "whether tangible or visible, is not so properly an object [*i.e.*, in the present connection, matter of sensation] as a necessary concomitant of the objects both of sight and touch." Space, it is true, "seems not to enter at first into the mind until it is introduced by the proper objects of sense;" it is "not perceived by any of our senses when all matter is removed." But "when we perceive any of the primary qualities, *space presents itself as a necessary concomitant*."[1] Reid also recognises space as the source of a necessity which sense cannot give. Kant's statements on this point have their parallels in passages like the following: "Some of the determinations we form concerning matter cannot be deduced solely from the testimony of sense, but must be referred to some other source. There seems to be nothing more evident than that all bodies must consist of parts; and that every part of a body is a body, and a distinct being, which may exist without the other parts; and yet I apprehend this conclusion is not deduced solely from the testimony of sense; for,

[1] Works, p. 324.

besides that it is a necessary truth, and therefore no object of sense, there is a limit beyond which we cannot perceive any division of a body. The parts become too small to be perceived by our senses; but we cannot believe that it becomes then incapable of being further divided, or that such a division would make it not to be a body." "There are other determinations concerning matter, which, I think, are not solely founded upon the testimony of sense: such as, that it is impossible that two bodies should occupy the same place at the same time; or that the same body should be in different places at the same time; or that a body can be moved from one place to another without passing through the intermediate places, either in a straight course or by some circuit. These appear to be necessary truths, and therefore cannot be conclusions of our senses; for our senses testify only what is, and not what must necessarily be."[1]

On the *second* point—his insistence on judgment as the unit of knowledge—Reid again occupies the same position as Kant, who, it will be remembered, makes judgment the badge of objectivity in cognition, and professes accordingly to deduce his table of the categories from an

[1] Works, pp. 323, 324.

analysis of the act of judgment. Reid's unguarded talk about a knowledge of the sensations *per se* may be pardoned in view of still more serious lapses on Kant's part. For the rest, Reid states his position in the broadest possible way. He denies, as we have seen, the possibility of a start with subjective sensations, or what he calls "simple apprehension." We do not begin by studying the contents of our own minds, and afterwards proceed by inference to realities beyond. This course, he sees clearly, leads inevitably to scepticism. Once cooped up within these limits, we only wait for Hume to make us logical. But the correct "anatomy of the mind" does not bear out such presuppositions. We are never restricted to our own ideas; from the first, we are in the presence of reality. "Every operation of the senses, in its very nature, implies judgment or belief, as well as simple apprehension."[1] First of these judgments of nature must be taken the implication in every thought or sensation of a permanent subject of thought. But the natural judgments which constitute the apparently simple sensation are not exhausted by this single reference. "Sensation suggests the notion of present existence." "When I perceive a tree before me,

Works, p. 209.

my faculty of seeing gives me not only a notion or simple apprehension of the tree, but a belief of its existence; and this judgment or belief is not got by comparing ideas, it is included in the very nature of the perception."[1] This judgment of existence, seemingly too obvious to require mention, and which Hume, as already remarked, endeavoured to confound with the impressions themselves, is yet found, on analysis and careful consideration, to be the root of the whole matter. The definite judgment of existence by which any impression is, so to speak, transfixed, and stopped in its fleeting course, carries with it the idea of an object—that is, in germ, a real world to which we are related, and of which we have, in Reid's language, an irresistible and necessary belief, or, as we might say without harm, an immediate consciousness or perception. Ego and Non-Ego both emerge in that judgment, and are locked together by it. For we must not suppose that the judgment of existence comes *after* the reference to a subject. Reid himself binds us to no such order; and we ought to guard ourselves, above all things, against importing the idea of chronological succession into an analysis of knowledge. For in a real sense, it may be

[1] Works, p. 209.

said that one such judgment involves and contains all.

Recognition of existence, then, means fixation. The sensation, if we still call it so, has become invested with permanency; it is a percept, an object. Though it is mine, yet it is not me, in that it has relations to a whole real world, of which it is the result, and of which I as yet know nothing, except the fact that I am somehow related to it. A knowledge of what the further relations of the real are, is acquired by the application of further judgments which are latent in the first or primary judgment. It was the newness and unusualness of my state, it may be surmised, which first led me to concentrate attention upon it and fix it as existent. But this very curiosity involved the desire to know whence it came, how it came to pass—in other words, its cause. By a more explicit application of the causal judgment, therefore, I seek to connect my sensation with some change in the objects around me; I connect the smell (to take Reid's former example) with the presence of a visible and tactual object called a rose. Here, again, I am employing a principle which is not derivable from experience or comparison of ideas, but is involved in the genesis of experience as such. In course of time, as my thinking becomes more capable of abstract distinctions, I separate the different aspects of the rose in thought, and affirm them all, as qualities, of the rose, as substance. Once more, however, we may note that the determination of any quality as a quality is implicit in the first challenge of the sensation—in the refusal to let it pursue its own transitory existence, floating over the surface of an animal sentiency, unexplaining and unexplained. By that challenge, the notion of reality is once for all constituted for the mind; there emerges for consciousness the notion of a real world—the notion of permanence and change. This contrast lies in the most elementary judgment of differentiation, in which consciousness might be figured as arising. It is because we cannot regard each moment as sufficient unto itself, that we are betrayed into explanation — into connecting the sensitive and transient content with an existence at least relatively permanent and self-subsistent. Such a reference is, in slightly different forms, the judgment of substantiality and the judgment of causality; and these are the chief levers in the interpretation of nature. In very deed, and perhaps in a deeper sense than Reid meant his words, these are "natural judgments"—"judgments immediately inspired by our constitution"—for the self-conscious being does simply convey into such judgments his own "constitution"—the self-explaining contrasts of his own nature—unity in multiplicity and permanence in change.

The last sentence suggests a word or two in conclusion as to the ultimate nature of *explanation*, in regard to which a good deal of misconception seems current. Reid says on one occasion that, in the last resort, "we know as little how we perceive as how we are made."[1] He is combating certain metaphorical explanations of the perceptive process, which in reality explain nothing; and his curt words convey a truth which may be more generally expressed. We are what we are, as Butler says, and we can give no reason for our own nature—*i.e.*, for the nature of self-consciousness; we can simply analyse it, and state its constitution, as accurately as may be. Accordingly, when we have placed any connection of matter of fact on the same footing as the fundamental relations in which our own life consists, we have done all that we can be expected to do. Yet the views which are perhaps most widely current almost exactly reverse what has just

[1] Works, p. 302.

been said. There are many, like Mill, who, when driven, by innate candour and the stress of logic combined, to admit certain undeniable facts of our conscious life,[1] still insist upon treating that life as (in their own words) a final inexplicability —that is to say, a solitary riddle left unread among the generally well-explained phenomena of nature. Self-consciousness is presented by such thinkers as the exception to the general course of things—the one lock that cannot be fitted, instead of being itself the key which opens to us all the wards of the universe. Its essential nature is spoken of by one writer as a "peculiarity," which makes it hopelessly "intractable and puzzling" to deal with; another refers to its leading characteristic as a "curious fact." Mysterious enough, if you will, but not curious. A curious fact is something out of the way, something unexpectedly stumbled upon in the midst of a smoothly-going scheme of things; and such a phrase implies a fundamental misconception of the nature of explanation and the limits of its possibility. And a similar confusion is observable in all the attempts, so widely current, to explain higher or more complex facts by exhibiting their genesis out of simpler conditions. As science,

[1] Examination of Hamilton, chap. xii.

such explanations are in their proper place, and are at once interesting and valuable; but, when put forward as philosophy, they simply invert the true point of view. Philosophical explanation must always set out from the highest term of the series; in any ultimate statement of the nature of that which is, the lower must be explained by the higher, and not *vice versâ*. All other explanation explains away, and is no better than the attempt to get something out of nothing. All principles of explanation, accordingly, are derived, and must be derived, from the nature of the explaining Self; they are transcripts, so to speak, of its own constitution. To seek to penetrate beyond this is really, as Lotze sometimes quaintly puts it, wishing to know how being is made.

## LECTURE IV.

### REID AND KANT.

In the preceding Lecture, two points were signalised in which a parallel might be drawn between Reid's work and the work of Kant. It remains for us to see how far, having regard to other aspects of Reid's philosophy, we are justified in maintaining a comparison between the two men.

We may best begin by considering Reid's account of the principles which he declares to be essential to the very existence of knowledge. As regards the nomenclature which he adopts, it may be admitted, at the outset, that the name "Principles of Common Sense" is unfortunate on account of its misleading associations—associations which have been strengthened rather than weakened by the unguarded utterances of its champions. The term is misleading, because it confounds philosophy and life. No doubt the end of a true philosophy is to justify ordinary knowledge and practice — that is, to state and harmonise the principles on which they rest. So far as a philosophy fails to do this—so far as it abolishes distinctions and principles that are actually present in life—we must agree with Reid that such a system is "at war with the common-sense of mankind." We must conclude that it is an inadequate, one-sided, and therefore fallacious, system. But though philosophy is thus ultimately to be judged by its accordance with life, the two must always remain essentially separate. They move on different planes. Life, whether knowing or doing, is a direct process. It is the primary fact—the object under examination. Philosophy is reflection upon life — a process wholly secondary and indirect. They differ as any process differs from the theory of the process. We may do without philosophy, if we will; but we cannot make common-sense, in the ordinary acceptation of the term, take its place and do its work. Now this fundamental distinction is often obscured by the language of the Scottish philosophers. This is fully admitted by Hamilton, even in the act of defending the argument from

Common Sense as truly philosophical. "It must be allowed," he says, "that the way in which it has been sometimes applied was calculated to bring it into not unreasonable disfavour with the learned. . . . Some of those who opposed it to the sceptical conclusions of Hume did not sufficiently counteract the notion which the name might naturally suggest; they did not emphatically proclaim that it was no appeal to the undeveloped beliefs of the unreflective many; and they did not inculcate that it presupposed a critical analysis of these beliefs by the philosophers themselves. On the contrary, their language and procedure might even sometimes warrant an opposite conclusion."[1] But when this is once said, perhaps there is nothing to be got by harping further upon it; for, in spite of some almost inexcusable passages, there is no doubt that Reid would have admitted the truth of the distinction that has just been made. He is much too fond of opposing "the vulgar" to the tribe of philosophers — to "all philosophers, ancient and modern," as he goes the length of saying on one occasion. But it is always, more or less, a point with philosophers to demonstrate the harmony of their doctrine with the common beliefs of men.

[1] Reid's Works, p. 752.

We need only recall Berkeley's very similar references to philosophers as a body, and his assurances, for example, that since his "revolt from metaphysical notions to the plain dictates of nature and common-sense, he found his understanding strangely enlightened"[1]—in order to judge Reid's utterances more leniently. But even if we put the worst possible construction upon his words, his own action sufficiently belies them. He proceeds to undertake that very critical analysis of consciousness which, according to his supposed principles, would have been unnecessary. Does he apologise for doing so? On the contrary, he undertakes the analysis unhesitatingly, as a matter of course; and, in spite of his hard words about philosophers, he claims to take his place as one of them. In writing to Hume about his own 'Inquiry,' for example, he avows himself Hume's "disciple in metaphysics," and speaks of himself as "attempting to throw some new light on these abstruse subjects." These are not the words of a man who deems philosophy superfluous, inasmuch as it may be picked up from every rustic. In truth, the opposition emphasised by Reid is not

---

[1] A number of similar expressions are quoted from Berkeley by Reid (Works, p. 283), and every reader of Berkeley will recall many more.

properly between Common Sense and Philosophy, but between the "Philosophy of Common Sense" and all previous philosophies. More particularly, the antagonism lies between the Philosophy of Common Sense and the prevailing drift of modern philosophy, which Reid named the ideal system. It is because philosophers in general seemed to him, in adopting that system, to have divorced themselves from reality, that we hear so much in Reid of the opposition between philosophy and the common consciousness of man. As Hamilton puts it, the argument from common-sense, in Reid's hands, "is only an appeal from the heretical conclusions of particular philosophers to the catholic principles of all philosophy."[1]

But in order to be convinced of the close relationship which subsists between Reid's principles and those which are elsewhere offered, under more imposing titles, for our acceptance, it is only necessary to turn to some of the other names and descriptions of them which he gives in different parts of his writings. In the preface to the 'Inquiry,' he couples common-sense at once with reason ("the common-sense and reason of mankind"); and this is never retracted. If, at one point,[2] first principles are expressly excluded

[1] Reid's Works, p. 751.   [2] Ibid., p. 108.

from the province of reason, that is because, in the context, "reason" is equivalent to the modern "reasoning" or the discursive faculty; and what is intended is simply to assert the self-evident character of first principles, which renders them incapable of proof.[1] Throughout the 'Inquiry' there is no special account of the nature of the principles beyond their designation—and that is highly important—as judgments. They are referred to as original and natural judgments, as judgments of nature, as simple and original principles of our constitution, and so forth—the term principles of common-sense remaining the favourite. In the 'Essays,' however, there is a fuller and maturer treatment of this point. Here there is less frequent use of the term common-sense, the principles being generally spoken of simply as

[1] In a fine passage of the 'Essays,' Reid repeats this very distinction, while emphatically asserting, in the same breath, the inseparable union of the two. "It is absurd to conceive that there can be any opposition between reason and common-sense. It is indeed the first-born of Reason; and as they are commonly joined together in speech and in writing, they are inseparable in their nature. We ascribe to reason two offices, or two degrees. The first is to judge of things self-evident; the second to draw conclusions that are not self-evident from those that are. The first of these is the province, and the sole province, of common-sense; and, therefore, it coincides with reason in its whole extent, and is only another name for one branch or one degree of reason."—Works, p. 425.

"first principles" or "common principles." In his official chapter on "First Principles in General," in the Essay on Judgment, Reid describes them as "intuitive judgments," "self-evident principles," "propositions which are no sooner understood than they are believed." Each "has the light of truth in itself, and has no occasion to borrow it from another"; and he quotes with approbation Shaftesbury's incidental designation of them as "natural knowledge, fundamental reason, and common-sense." These terms may take their place without shame alongside of Kant's pure reason, his principles of pure understanding, his categories or root-conceptions, his principles of synthesis *a priori*.

To Reid, as to Kant, his principles are the source of a necessity which sense, as sense, cannot give. But if we ask any further reason for the principles themselves, Reid wisely answers that they are "a part of our constitution," "a part of that furniture which nature hath given to the human understanding"; or, if we prefer the term, we may justly call them "the inspiration of the Almighty." "No reasons can be given for original principles but the Will of our Maker." Neither does Kant profess to prove why our pure perceptions and categories are what they are.

The transcendental proof of the principles faces entirely towards experience; it proves that, if we take any portion of actual experience to pieces, we shall find that it is held together, so to speak, by the presence of these elements. But if we care to raise a further question, no proof can possibly be offered why experience, or, to put it more broadly, why reason, why God, should not have had a totally different nature. The question itself is idle.

But the mention of the transcendental deduction suggests an important point in which Reid is usually thought—and, as we shall see, not without reason—to compare unfavourably with Kant. What proof does Reid offer of the *necessity*—*i.e.*, the *indispensableness*—of these principles, which he adduces as ultimate, and refers to the constitution of the mind? It is commonly said, to his discredit, that he offers none,—that it is simply matter of assertion with him, an appeal to intuition—that is, to an unverifiable subjective consciousness. Hume had shown, by a deduction from principles accepted among philosophers, that certain beliefs had no warrant, and had thereby explained away certain existences, such as mind and matter, which are usually taken for granted. In answer to this, it would seem, according to a current account of the affair, as if Reid had simply cried in the streets, so to speak, asseverating that, *in spite of philosophy,* he found a guarantee of these realities and principles within his breast, and that he was determined to hold to them. To which Hume, of course, could always answer, with a tinge of compassion, that certainly there was no harm in keeping the beliefs, and acting upon them—as he himself, for the matter of that, was fully prepared to do—but that really, so far as philosophy was concerned, this was in no sense a relevant answer, so long as the reasoning remained unattacked, which, by laying bare their origin, had destroyed their warrant. This is substantially the idea which Kant had of Reid and the Scottish philosophers, and it has been too readily accepted by those who represent the German influence in British philosophy. Reid has doubtless had to suffer in part for the sins of the lesser men who took up the cry against Hume. Undoubtedly, too, he frequently gives occasion himself to the enemy, by the way in which he parades the opposition between philosophy and common-sense. For although we may grant to Reid that, in a certain sense, ridicule, as he often says, may be a test of truth, yet the clumsy and ineffective ridicule with which he sometimes assails the sceptical position resembles too closely Dr Johnson's rough-and-ready refutation of Berkeley, and inevitably suggests to unfriendly readers a misapprehension of the philosophic position. Ridicule is a weapon which should be sparingly used in philosophical discussion. It is so easy to make sport for the Philistines, seeing that any philosophic position whatever must wear a look of unreality to those who are content to live among the things of sense. Thought, as such, or the ultimate statement of any fact, has a flavour of absurdity to the man who does not think. Reid is not to be defended, therefore, so far as he resorts to this unworthy philosophical horse-play. But such passages are not the essential parts of Reid. It has been seen that, so far from meeting Hume's conclusion by an unsupported reassertion of what was there sceptically explained away, Reid, admitting the formal correctness of the reasoning, set on foot a rigorous investigation into the premisses or assumptions on which the conclusion depended, by way of discovering whether there did not lurk in these some root of falsity, which vitiated all that followed. No procedure could be more distinctively philosophical than this. And we have seen that he found this root of falsity in the ideal system.

The ultimate elements of knowledge are not detached ideas or states of consciousness; "natural and original judgments" alone make experience possible. In Kantian language, mere sense is an abstraction; and therefore we cannot make a start with it in explaining knowledge.

Yet it must be admitted that, in this matter of proof, Reid does fall short of Kant. "By attending to the operations of thinking, memory, reasoning, we perceive or judge," he says, "that there must be something which thinks, remembers, and reasons, which we call the mind."[1] But he never fairly explains the reason of this "must." We need only compare Reid's statement with Kant's deduction of the unity of apperception, in order to be aware of the difference. A permanent subject, Kant argues, is necessary even for the comparison of two sensations, even for the passage from one moment of time to the next; experience would fall to pieces without it. To draw a line, even, implies consciousness of the first parts as we go on to the next. Without the reference to a permanent Self, as principle of synthesis, the line would fall asunder into numberless punctual dots; the first being forgotten before the second came on the

Works, p. 421.

scene, so that each, in its turn, would be for us a perpetual first. But experience is not of this sieve-like character; accordingly, to explain our actual experience—*i.e.*, to account for its being what it is—a permanent Self becomes a necessary assumption. Such is the essence of the transcendental deduction—the proof by reference to the possibility of experience. It essays no absolute (or abstract) proof of the principles or categories. It does not profess to show that experience must be as it is; but, taking experience as a fact, it proves that we could not have *such* an experience without the presence of certain principles. There is nothing difficult, and surely nothing mystical, about the proof. It is the time-honoured logical *reductio per impossibile*. Withdraw the rivets, it says, and experience tumbles to pieces. Suppose the principles absent, and follow up the supposition into its consequences; you will find that the result does not tally with reality, and cannot, indeed, be stated in terms of thought. How very near Reid came to the spirit of such an argument, may be seen from his remarks (Sixth Essay, c. 4) on first principles, and the nature of the proof they admit of. "It may be observed," he says, "that although it is contrary to the nature of first principles to admit of direct or apodictical proof, yet there are certain ways of reasoning even about them, by which those that are just and solid may be confirmed, and those that are false may be detected. First, it is a good argument *ad hominem*, if it can be shown that a first principle which a man rejects, stands upon the same footing with others which he admits. . . . Secondly, a first principle may admit of a proof *ad absurdum*. In this kind of proof, which is very common in mathematics, we suppose the contradictory proposition to be true. We trace the consequences of that supposition in a train of reasoning; and if we find any of its necessary consequences to be manifestly absurd, we conclude the supposition from which it followed to be false, and therefore its contradictory to be true."[1] The general statement of the argument is there, but there is wanting the luminous application of it, which alone constitutes the real discovery of a method. We look in vain in Reid for anything that could, with any strictness of language, be called an application of the method of proof here enunciated. Certainly he does not, like Kant, make it the point on which his entire system turns.

[1] Works, p. 439.

When Reid does offer any proof of his principles, he has recourse by predilection to the argument from universality of acceptance—the *quid facti*, which Kant stigmatises as carrying with it no certificate of validity. His favourite appeal is to common-sense, "where every man is a competent judge"—to "the consent of ages and nations, of the learned and unlearned."[1] As regards this argument, however, which has drawn upon Reid so much opprobrium from succeeding philosophers, it is only fair to add that his way of putting it is not always so unphilosophical as is generally supposed. The objections to this mode of arguing are, in the first place, that it is the acceptance of a verdict from those who have never learned to reflect; and secondly, that it is impossible to get at anything like a really universal consensus of opinion, or to reach, with any certainty, the actual contents and structure of the uncorrupted consciousness. Reid, however, does not leave his authority so vague; he provides his scattered and inarticulate multitude with an accredited spokesman and interpreter. "We shall frequently have occasion," he says in the beginning of the 'Essays,' "to argue from the sense of mankind *expressed in the struc-*

[1] Works, p. 439.

*ture of language."* [1] This line of argument does not occur in the 'Inquiry,' but throughout the 'Essays' the argument from common-sense is almost identified with this appeal to "the structure and grammar of all languages." "The structure of all languages," he says, "is grounded upon common notions." The distinction, for example, "between sensible qualities and the substance, to which they belong, and between thought and the mind that thinks, is not the invention of philosophers; it is found in the structure of all languages, and therefore must be common to all men who speak with understanding." [2] Here we have, at all events, an incorruptible witness, and one that will abide our questions. And if we reflect upon the closeness of the connection between grammar and the Aristotelian logic, the argument has manifest affinities with Kant's deduction of the categories from the forms of judgment. In neither case have we, strictly speaking, a proof of the principles. What we have is, in Kant's language, rather a *clue* to the discovery of principles, which require afterwards the transcendental proof.

It is the presence and conscious application of this latter proof that gives Kant his chief

[1] Works, p. 233.   [2] Ibid., pp. 229, 454.

advantage over his Scottish contemporary. At all events, it is the transcendental deduction that has played the most important part in the arguments of the English Kantio-Hegelians. This is the pivot on which Green's famous 'Introduction to Hume' turns; and it is beyond doubt that the vital part of Kant's achievement may be all gathered round this one centre. Whatever is not covered by this proof is mere padding, or architectonic display. But, in comparing Kant with Reid, it must not be forgotten that Kant's followers—his English followers especially—have transformed his doctrine. It is a serious mistake to suppose that, in Green, for example, we have simply a revival of Kant, or a revival of Hegel, or a combination of the two. Materials certainly have been drawn from both these thinkers; but the result is a type of thought which has never existed before, and of which it is absurd, therefore, to speak as an importation from Germany. It has been developed within the shadow of, and with special reference to, the 'Treatise of Human Nature'—a book which was practically unknown to the great German thinkers. Its method is Kantian, and it uses Hegel only as a means of surmounting Kant's subjective presuppositions, leaving on one side the technicalities of the

Hegelian system. But it is far more thorough-going than Kant; and it is hardly paradoxical to say that, if we take Reid at his strongest and best, the broad sweep of his protest against independent ideas bears a very close resemblance to Green's massive argument against unrelated impressions. The resemblance is even closer, one might almost say, than that which exists between Green and the general tenor of the 'Critique of Pure Reason.' For Kant had only Hume's 'Inquiry' before him, and we know that it was simply Hume's analysis of causality which first roused his critical reflection. Moreover, if the truth must be confessed, *Kant does not himself consistently employ the proof* which he so brilliantly states, and which he ostensibly makes the lever of his whole investigation. Even in the very section in which he states the principle of a transcendental deduction, he excepts the categories from its operation, and thereby deprives his theory of its only solid foundation. The evidence of this will occupy us presently.

Meanwhile it only remains to sum up the general results of this survey of Reid's work, undertaken in view of the parallel achievement of Kant. Besides the defective proof, it must be freely admitted that Reid's enumeration of principles is neither so full nor so methodical as Kant's. He had not the latter's passion for architectonics and finality. Not that there did not hover before Reid's eyes too the ideal of "a system of the mind," which should consist, in Kant's language, of "an inventory, systematically arranged, of all that is given us by pure reason."[1] "A clear explication and enumeration of the principles of common-sense," he says, in concluding his first work, "is one of the chief *desiderata* in logic."[2] But his estimate of his own achievement, both then and in his later work, was characteristically modest: "If the enumeration should appear to some redundant, to others deficient, and to others both—if things which I conceive to be first principles should to others appear to be vulgar errors, or to be truths which derive their evidence from other truths, and therefore not first principles,—in these things every man must judge for himself. I shall rejoice to see an enumeration more perfect in any or in all of these respects."[3] These are not altogether suitable words in a philosopher's mouth; but I fear no one can read over what Reid calls "first principles of contingent

---

[1] Critique of Pure Reason, First Preface.
[2] Works, p. 209.          [3] Ibid., p. 441.

truth," without judging that he has really fallen into both the faults he mentions, and into the additional one of bad arrangement. The truth is, Reid's lack of form, and his frequent want of precision in statement, have militated fatally, from the first, against his being ranked as a philosophical classic. The difference between Reid and Kant in this respect is striking. Though Kant's style is involved, his terminology often cumbrous, and his works abounding in repetitions, yet he mingles no extraneous and strictly indifferent matter with his argument. In each of his great works there is the sense of a unity of aim which the repetitions only serve to make more prominent. On the other hand, Reid's properly philosophical positions are imbedded in a mass of irrelevant psychological matter-of-fact, which obscures their bearing and impairs their force. Kant and Reid were both university professors, but their method of working was different. Reid's books, especially his later 'Essays,' are in the main his lectures prepared for publication; and they are marked, therefore, by a greater diffuseness and by a more popular character than we have a right to expect in a written treatise. Kant, on the other hand, appears to have made a rigid distinction between his work as a university teacher, and his work as a regenerator of philosophy. The latter was addressed not to students and general readers, but to teachers and to a learned public. If, as the story goes, not actually written down with the care which a *magnum opus* might be supposed to demand, no labour had been spared in working out the plan and phraseology of the 'Critique' with a precision worthy of its destination. Reid wrote no *magnum opus*, in the sense in which Kant wrote several. He had no learned class to whom he could have appealed, if he had written with the elaborate technicality of Kant. His works were addressed to the reading portion of his countrymen generally—to his old students, in great part, and the ministers of religion, into whose ranks many of them had doubtless passed. The *Fachmann*, or specialist, has hitherto not flourished among us, and the disadvantages of his absence are obvious. But it is possible that what Scottish philosophy has lost in scientific precision may have been compensated for, in part, by the greater influence which it has exerted upon the body of the people—an influence which has made it a factor, so to speak, in the national life. It is matter of history, on the other hand, that the great idealistic movement in Germany in the beginning of this century passed entirely over the heads of the German people. It passed away, leaving the ground clear for a variety of crude materialistic theories. The so-called Kantian revival, of which so much has been heard of late, where not merely philological, has been for the most part a popularising of Kant's Agnostic results. Hegel's philosophy has had a wide, and frequently unobserved, influence in moulding many departments of thought; but, *as philosophy*, it never lived in Germany beyond the confines of the schools. It spoke in an unknown tongue, and the people were not edified; it may be said to have died of its technical dialect. Of course the mass of the people cannot be philosophers, any more than they can be experts in any science. But philosophy, just because it discusses subjects of such momentous import, lies nearer to their hearts than any science of detail can do; and therefore things cannot be altogether healthy, when there is no manner of touch whatever between the many and the few. The many are sure in that case to be left a prey to superficial crudities, or to practical materialism.

But be that as it may, Reid's candid acknowledgment of his imperfections may be accepted in good part. His deficiencies and redundancies ought not to make us overlook what is really to be found in his works. It behoves us rather to gather together what is valuable, and to give it its proper setting. This is partly what we have been trying to do. We have now to turn to Kant, in order to consider his system shortly as a whole.

The leverage here also was supplied by Hume; and the form in which the question was taken up by Kant was that of the possibility of necessary connection. Kant could not doubt that necessary connection is a fact. But Hume had just shown that this necessity could not be given by sense; and following up this proof, he had dissolved our knowledge into particular perceptions, whose connections were purely contingent and customary. Kant adopts Hume's position on the first point. Sense, he argues, cannot give necessity; and he identifies sense with that of which we are passively recipient—with that which comes to us from the object. From this Kant concludes that, *if* our perceptions are wholly due to sense—*if* we are wholly limited to contributions from the object,—there can be no other necessity than the custom-bred semblance of it which Hume offers. If, on the contrary, we hold by necessity (as the facts compel us to do), it must come from some other source—from the only other possible source,

the subject. This is Kant's Copernican idea.
Granted that a world of mere sense would be a
huddle of contingent units, this unlimited contingency is not the world we know. The world we
know must, therefore, be dependent for its principles of necessary connection—*i.e.*, for its most
important determinations or characteristics—upon
the knowing mind. The human mind is not the
humble satellite of things that it was formerly supposed to be; on the contrary, objects, as we know
them, draw from the mind, as from a central
source, those principles of rational connection that
make them knowable. For example, it is beyond
doubt that we recognise objects in space—*i.e.*, as
outside of one another, and as consisting of parts
that are outside of one another; and the extension
of bodies is, so to speak, the basal quality on
which the other qualities are superimposed. The
placedness of objects, moreover, is something over
and above the qualitative difference of one sensation from another; it is something different in
kind, and cannot be given by any series of
sensations as such. We must not speak, therefore, of generating space out of impressions. No
cunning mixture of impressions, with whatever
rapidity and regularity they may follow one
another, could give us more than just so many

impressions. Space or externality, accordingly, is a condition of the possibility of objects, to be carefully distinguished from the prick of sense, on occasion of which it is presented to the mind. And, as the prick of sense is all that is attributed by Kant to the object, he naturally concludes that space must be presented to the mind by the mind's self, of its own initiative and on its own authority. Space is the mind's "form" or mode of perception. In other words, the fundamental determination of the external world, as such, is due to a subjective projection from the perceiving mind—a subjective net, in Dr Stirling's phrase, thrown, as it were, by the mind to catch impressions.

When we pass to the categories, or connective principles of the understanding, the procedure is the same, or at least it is the same in one aspect of Kant's teaching. Prominent among these notions or principles, it will be remembered, are those of substance and cause, which Hume had left as a problem, and with which we found Reid also busying himself. Without these principles and others, it is impossible to construct experience as we know it. Objects are objects solely in virtue of their presence; or, in Kant's language, perceptions without notions are blind. But the principles or notions cannot be given

I

by sense; therefore they must be infused into sense by the mind. A chaos (Gewühl) of phenomena might fill the sense-dependent soul, but without notions no cognition could arise: notions are, as it were, the threads of connection which the mind shoots through the chaos. Sense, as sense, would, according to Kant, be a mere blur—a manifold, not even recognised *as* a manifold. In short, to have the cognition of objects in space, as we do in point of fact perceive them, we must add to sense the pure forms of perception (time and space), the judgments or principles of pure understanding (the categories), and, as presupposed in all, the unity of apperception, which grasps everything in one consciousness or one world. Each of these elements is an abstraction without the other — that is, they are incapable of separate realisation. You cannot have impressions without simultaneously proceeding to arrange them in space and time; and you cannot have space and time without the categories, for you construct space and time by means of active synthesis, and the categories are the principles of that synthesis. Nor can you have the Ego apart from its act of synthesis: to speak paradoxically, it creates itself and its object by, and in the course of, the same synthetical act. At no point can this circle of mutual presupposition be broken.

The synthesis effected by the unity of apperception in the jumble of particulars, is what Kant calls the synthesis of apprehension or of imagination — *synthesis speciosa*. And he says at one point explicitly that all synthesis,— such, even, as makes perception or apprehension (Wahrnehmung) possible,—must be subjected to the conditions of the categories (unter den Kategorien); and again, the imaginative synthesis is expressly said to take place according to the categories (den Kategorien gemäss).[1] The synthesis of the imagination must be, indeed, in consistency, just the synthesis of the understanding *in action*. The categories are the Ego's modes of judgment, its forms of connection. Its nature is expressed in them, or reflected into them; and through them it realises itself. It cannot combine and connect except through its own forms of combination and connection; and, as it is only through such synthesis that it is itself actual, the Ego is manifestly inseparable from the categories. This is what Kant would seem bound by his own principles to say; and at some points — as in the passages quoted above

[1] Werke, iii. 127 (ed. Hartenstein, 1868).

—he certainly does appear to say it. Accordingly some of his interpreters have presented this as the consistent Kantian doctrine, treating irreconcilable utterances as mere incidental fallings-away on Kant's part. But the mass of irreconcilable statements is too great to be so treated, and Kant's final deliverances are, unfortunately, directly opposed to the consistent theory outlined above. The reason of this failure in consistency will probably become apparent, if we keep the theory steadily in view, and examine the consequences in which it involves us.

We must remember, then, that the constructive elements of the world, not being found in sense as sense, have been referred to a mental or subjective source. Therefore, although we have a cosmos or world before us, that world is not the real world; it is not the world we set out to know. It is, in part, an effect of the world of real existence; but we cannot by any conceivable possibility tell how the world of knowledge—which we may henceforth call the phenomenal world—stands related to the world of reality, or, as Kant calls it, the noumenal world. We have vindicated rationality and necessity of connection for our universe; and we have now a cosmos, or nature, in which science can work.

But this has been achieved at a terrible cost. For we have to bear in mind that, without exception, as Kant puts it, the objects we are dealing with are "not things-in-themselves, but the mere play of our ideas, which in the end are merely determinations of the internal sense."[1] "All objects without exception with which we busy ourselves are *in me*—that is, are determinations or modes of my identical self."[2] Hence, though it seems paradoxical and absurd to speak of the understanding as prescribing laws *a priori* to nature, the wonder ceases, according to Kant, if we reflect "that this nature is itself nothing but a sum of phenomena—not a thing-in-itself, therefore, but only a number of subjective ideas (eine Menge von Vorstellungen des Gemüths).[3] The subjective derivation of law is, indeed, a matter of course; for Kant explicitly tells us that, "as mere ideas, [phenomena] are subject to no law of connection except that which the connecting or synthetic faculty prescribes."[4]

"*As mere ideas*—'Vorstellungen' or mental facts—*they are subject to no law of their own.*" Is this true? Is the contribution from the side of the object this mere manifold or chaos

[1] Werke, iii. 569.
[2] Ibid., p. 585.
[3] Ibid., p. 576.
[4] Ibid., pp. 133, 134.

—this jumble of unconnected and mutually indifferent particulars? Do we really introduce a subjective, and to that extent arbitrary, order into this objective chaos, thus working up a formless material into a coherent world? Evidently, such a conception of the attitude of the individual subject to the influences which reality brings to bear upon him is not tenable for a moment. Nor does Kant himself attempt to maintain that the given "matter" is pure matter or unlimited contingency. He admits that "empirical laws as such can in no wise derive their origin from the pure understanding — as little, indeed, as the boundless multiplicity of phenomena can be sufficiently understood from the pure form of sense-perception."[1] In other words, the given matter *has* laws of its own, to begin with. We cannot weave it into any phantasmagoria we please; we are determined in its regard —bound down to follow a certain course in our construction of sense-objects. To a large extent, at all events, our task is merely to read off what is there in the material, waiting to be deciphered. "But all empirical laws," Kant proceeds, "are only particular determinations or applications of the pure laws of the understanding."[2] If

[1] Werke, iii. 583.  [2] Ibid., p. 584.

this is the case, as reflection shows it must be, why may we not go a step further, and evolve the general law from the particular cases of it furnished by the empirical data? What necessity is there for the appeal to a subjective source at all?

This point is admirably pressed home by Dr Stirling in his 'Text-book to Kant,' and elsewhere.[1] I have stated above the view of Kant's theory, which makes him, in a way, consistent with himself. This view has been worked out more particularly by English thinkers, who use Kant as an instrument of philosophy rather than exactly state the Kantian system. The few passages which, if rigorously interpreted, may be taken as supporting such a view, are put completely out of sight by the mass of evidence which proves Kant himself to have held a very different-complexioned theory. Objects, Kant says, may quite well be given to us in space and time independently of the action of the categories; they may certainly appear to us without any necessary reference to

[1] I hardly require to point out how much I am indebted to Dr Stirling throughout this account of Kant. Most of my readers will be aware of what I may call the Kantian campaign recently undertaken by our veteran metaphysician. Opened in the 'Journal of Speculative Philosophy,' it may be said to have been successfully concluded in the 'Text-book to Kant.' This has recently been followed by two articles in 'Mind,' under the title, "Kant has *not* answered Hume."

the functions of the understanding. Perception or intuition, merely as such, he says, has no need whatever of the functions of thought. In short, Kant does not take his own dictum rigorously, that perceptions without notions are blind. They are blind only in so far as they are, so to speak, not focussed. The intelligence, we might say, has not exerted itself about them—has not thrown itself upon them, and fixed them as such and such. It remains a kind of mirror for reality, much as the field of vision in the retina receives images—which, however, are only vaguely present till they are actively focussed or fixed at the centre of the field. Kant, as is his wont, has a special function to account for the information or perception so acquired. The synthesis of imagination, he says, " as a blind but indispensable function of the soul," must be held to precede the action of the understanding. Elsewhere he calls it the first synthesis of apprehension, which, as it were, runs through the units of sense, giving them continuity, and bringing to light, as we must suppose, the connections which really exist in the matter submitted. It is only when recognition is added to apprehension, he seems to say, that notions or categories come in. To this uncategorised perception—crude perception Dr Stirling calls it—Kant allows a wide range. Not only has imagination the preparatory work of laying out the units as a spatial and temporal manifold, ready for the action of the category, which is to strike them into unities or objects, and to bind these objects together in necessary bonds; Kant speaks, and speaks advisedly, of objects as already present to the mind before the categories act. We may perceive objects, and also connections between objects; but, he adds, it is *only perceiving*, in a narrower sense of that word. The result is only a judgment of perception—a statement of matter of fact, devoid of necessity. I have, for example, the perception of the sun and the perception of warmth in a stone, and I find that, as matter of fact, the second follows the first. So much I find by merely adding to the empirical data the perceptional forms of space and time; but the assertion of a dynamic or necessary connection between the two—the judgment that the one is actually the cause of the other—is only to be made, according to Kant, by bringing out the category, and stamping therewith this particular case of succession. Only thus do I reach cognition or *experience* in the narrower sense of that word, as opposed to perception. When I say, "the sun warms the stone," I have formulated a scientific or universally valid statement; in Kantian language, I have made a judgment of experience.

This is a most lame and impotent conclusion; but it has apparently been the result of much anxious thought on Kant's part. After the first publication of the 'Critique,' the question of causality in particular was evidently, as Dr Stirling puts it, the cause of many cold sweats to Kant. Between the first and the second edition, the consideration forced itself irresistibly upon him that there must be some *reason* why in *this* case of succession I bring forward the category of causality, whereas in another case I single out reciprocity, and in another, perhaps, am content with the categories of quantity. What guidance have I in employing now one category, now another? Evidently there is none in the categories themselves. They are ready, but indifferent; they await their summons. Whence does the summons come then? Whence can it come but from the sense-elements themselves — from the apprehended data? If, on perceiving the succession of the sun and the warm stone, I employ Causality, whereas, when I perceive in succession the top and the bottom of the façade of a house, I prefer to use Quantity, my choice must be due to some difference in the facts before me—a difference which I perceive, and which induces me to say that the one is a case of causality, the other of quantity. I *see* a causal order in the one case, a merely quantitative order in the other. But if the order is already there, why pretend to introduce it, as something entirely new, from the side of the subject? As Dr Stirling graphically puts it: " The category that is to be called out must have its appropriate cue. . . . The empirical variety itself must, . . . as it were, blow its own prompter's whistle before my judgment can be expected duly to subsume it into the appointed checker." The use to which Kant eventually puts the categories is, therefore, simply to add the mind's stamp of necessity to connections which exist independently, but which, as so existing, are *said* to be merely contingent. But it is no more than saying in both cases. If the connection is contingent, how can any action of mine make it necessary? If not because I see that the connection is necessary, how am I entitled to call it so? There seems, indeed, no reason whatever for saying that it is first contingent, and only afterwards necessary, except that otherwise the categories would find their occupation too palpably gone. Accordingly they have this ceremonial office conferred upon them.

The truth seems to be, as I have tried to put it elsewhere,[1] that Kant wavered between the view of sense as a chaotic manifold compelled into order by the individual's forms and categories, and the view of it as an empirically ordered manifold in which all determination belongs to the object, and is simply recognised by the subject. Only on the former view could the subjective machinery of the categories be of real use; and Kant's first thought apparently was that they functioned in that way. But the pressure of facts—nothing less than an incorrigible world of real connections—drove him speedily into the second position, which is summed up in the distinction already quoted from the 'Prolegomena' between judgments of perception and judgments of experience.

The categories, then, are useless, because they simply do over again what is already sufficiently done in the objects themselves; they merely automatically register what is there before them. May not the argument, however, have another turn given to it? Is not this demonstration of their uselessness and superfluity just another way of saying that, *because the categories are already in things*, we do not require subjectively to supply them?

[1] In a review of Dr Stirling's 'Text-book to Kant,' in 'Mind,' vii. 275.

Or, to put it otherwise, the data presented to us already involve the different forms of necessary and rational relatedness which the categories, as subjective functions, were invoked to supply. If this is so, Kant's work has not been altogether in vain. It is the old story of *The king is dead: long live the king!* As subjective functions, the categories are superfluous, but only because they live in the object. In this case, however, the given element must be something very different from what Kant supposed at the outset; reason and necessity enter into its very structure. Indeed, if we but reflect, it must strike us as an incongruous idea that this human mind of ours should, as it were, supply the defects of the world, and breathe into it principles of which it contains itself no hint. This is the fatal weakness of all theories which rest on innate ideas or intuitions of the mind; and the same subjective suggestion has obstinately clung to the term categories also, and even yet discredits those who use it. There is, it must unfortunately be admitted, too much reason for the bad odour it enjoys, when we consider its source in Kant. But as against all such conceptions of a subjective reason, experience is great, and will prevail. We must get rid, once for all, of the notion that the mind *adds* anything to things. To add is to disfigure, to distort, to betray. But the function of mind is to know things, and to know them as they are.

Our attitude, in short, towards the philosophy of Experience must entirely depend upon the meaning we put into the term Experience. Kant, it will have been observed, in joining issue with the Empiricists, accepts the Humian position on two important points: first, that the given element in knowledge is sensation; and secondly, that sensation is a mere contingent manifold, and can give no necessity. Hence, of course, there follows, in the third place, Kant's own expedien to save necessity; it must, on these terms, be the contribution of the mind in the process of knowing. But the attempt to carry out this new conception has had for Kant (or at least for us, viewing the spectacle of Kant's hopeless plungings) the result of refuting one of the premisses on which it depends. The given element is not to be identified with mere sensation or contingency. It yields to the knower objects and relations of objects, which are, to begin with, just what the categories are supposed afterwards to make them, and which, but for the shame of the thing, Kant would *call* rational and necessary.

And the argument formerly pressed home applies, it need hardly be added, along the whole line—to the pure perceptions of space and time no less than to the categories.[1] But if we make Experience, in this way, simply equivalent to the contribution of the object, then derivation from experience does not imply the absence of reason. It is a mistake to make any divorce, such as Kant makes, and timorous idealists are ever fond of making, between the contributions of the object and those of the subject, and to speak as if the latter possessed a higher value. To do so is to invite misconception; for the disproof of subjective origin, which is usually easy enough, is apt to be taken lightly as a disproof of the reason-constituted character of the facts in question. We ought to have no hesitation in proclaiming that we are all Experientialists, all Evolutionists. The point on which issue should be joined is the identification of Experience with mere sense. If we prove that this is not so, and that, on the contrary, mere sense is an abstraction impossible *in rerum naturâ*, Experientialism is at once shorn of all its supposed terrors.

[1] For, as definite location in space must be somehow given, if it is not to be purely arbitrary, there is *prima facie* no reason for supposing Space as a whole to be merely a subjective form.

And this, in my view, is the important point proved by the speculations of Kant and Reid alike. By neither is it stated with perfect clearness and consistency. But the proof is contained for us in Reid's distinction between Perception and Sensation, in his denial of a possible evolution of the one from the other, and in his exhibition of some at least of the Principles or Judgments involved in the former. It is also contained for us in Kant's demonstration that the essential constitution of objects involves the elements of space and time and the connections expressed by the categories, all of which are incapable of being given by sense as sense. In agreement so far, Reid and Kant part company entirely on the question of the reality of our knowledge, or what it is that we know. Having shown the baselessness of the accepted theory of ideas, which evolved an illusory objectivity out of subjective units, Reid felt that he had broken down the middle wall of partition which cut us off from reality; he felt entitled to claim an immediate knowledge of the real world. In Hamilton's phraseology, he was a Natural Realist. Kant, on the other hand, having rashly accepted from Hume the principle or prejudice that mere sense is all that can come from the object, took a very different course. Instead of, like Reid, abandoning "the ideal system," he elaborately reconstructed it, endeavouring to give it a more rational and tenable form. Kant is, indeed, the very prince of Representationists, and the Representationism of the present day has its roots almost entirely in the Kantian theory. But, in this respect, Kant must be considered to be *ultimus Romanorum*. The theory reached its final shape in his hands, and that shape dissolves away before a touch of criticism.

# LECTURE V.

### THE RELATIVITY OF KNOWLEDGE:
### KANT AND HAMILTON.

In agreement as to the reason-constituted character of our experience, Reid and Kant part company, as we have just seen, on the question of its relation to reality. And if the Scottish philosopher seems here in advance of the German, so far as the soundness and ultimate tenability of his position is concerned, the reason is that Reid had gone further than Kant in questioning the ideal system. In constructing his theory, Kant never questioned the fundamental assumption of that system, that we can know only our own ideas—Vorstellungen—or mental states. With Kant, then, as with Locke, our ideas, instead of bringing us into connection with things, really shut us off from them. But, with the analysis of Locke's successors in view, Kant does not find it possible to retain Locke's belief that the mental images literally represent or picture the nature of the real things. Extension, which was to Locke the clearest example of this mirroring of reality in the idea, is adduced by Kant as a demonstrative instance of that which cannot be derived from sensation at all, and which reflects, therefore, not the nature of things but only the nature of the mind. In proportion as Kant, having accepted Hume's proof of the impotence of sensation to yield connection, denudes the objective contribution of its permanent elements, and transfers them to the subject's side of the account—in the same proportion do the real things, which form the background in Locke's theory, become more and more shadowy. They become, indeed, in all strictness, an $x$—an unknown power to produce certain effects in us. The objectivity which Kant secures for experience is, therefore, only a *quasi* objectivity; it is a subjective objectivity, or an objectivity without reality. Kant's world is objective as compared with Hume's, in that it is lifted out of the flux of sensation and the accident of association by the presence of rational elements. But these elements (*because* they are not sensation, according to Kant's way of arguing) are merely subjective or mental. So that Kant's world is, after all, as little the real world we desiderate as Hume's; with either we remain Agnostics. And if that is so, it is comparatively indifferent whether our subjective world be hatched by the heating power of custom out of sense alone, or whether it is begotten of the union of sense with certain subjective forms of reason. This practical indifference is exemplified by many a would-be philosopher at the present day. In repudiating metaphysics, the sceptic or Agnostic finds it equally convenient to swear by Hume or by Kant; and it is almost a matter of accident which comes uppermost.

The Agnosticism, Phenomenalism, or Subjectivism, inherent in the Kantian theory, is sufficiently seen in the fruits it has borne, not only among men of general culture, but among professed adherents of the philosophic doctrine. Lange, the author of the 'History of Materialism,' is a typical example, and he has had a large following among the so-called Neo-Kantians of Germany. To Lange, and those who think with him, the great achievement of the 'Critique' is to have finally slain the chimeras of metaphysics, by fixing the limits of our necessary ignorance. And, of course, abundant evidence may be adduced to prove how strongly Kant's own mind was possessed by this view of his achievements; though it is only fair to add that, in such passages, where he speaks of the utility of the philosophy of pure reason as of an entirely negative character, Kant has usually in his mind the complementary function of the practical reason for which he is "making room." But this completion of the theory is, in general, rejected by the followers in question. They are content to abide by the negative results.

There is no necessity, however, to go so far afield for instances of the Agnostic tendency of the 'Critique.' Hamiltonianism shows, on the face of it, a mingling of Kantian and Scottish elements. I do not believe that there is any real fusion in Hamilton of these elements; nor need this astonish us, if we consider the incompatibility of the two doctrines. Any attempt to ingraft the Agnostic relativity of the 'Critique' upon the Natural Realism of the Scottish philosophy is, I hope to show, contrary to the genius of the latter. But anything I have to say on this point will be more intelligible and more in place after a consideration, on its merits, of the doctrine of the Relativity of Knowledge, as we find it both in Kant and Hamilton.

It is easy to trace the genesis of the doctrine in Kant's mind. It arose, as we have already seen, from his original identification of the "given" with mere sense, from his subsequent discovery that mere sense cannot give rational connection, and his consequent conclusion that such principles of connection must be supplied by the mind, or, in other words, that the fluid and indeterminate data of sense must be poured into certain mental moulds or faculties. The position is generalised by Kant in such passages as the following:—

"What may be the nature of objects, considered as things in themselves and without reference to the receptivity of our sensibility, is quite unknown to us. We know nothing more than our own mode of perceiving them, which is peculiar to us."

"Supposing that we should carry our empirical perception even to the very highest degree of clearness, we should not thereby advance a step nearer to a knowledge of the constitution of objects as things in themselves. For we could only, at best, arrive at a complete cognition of our own mode of perception, that is, of our sensibility."

"This receptivity of our faculty of cognition is called sensibility, and remains *toto cœlo* different from the cognition of an object in itself, and that even though we should look the phenomenon through and through to the very bottom."

"Everything in our knowledge that belongs to perception contains nothing more than relations, . . . and by means of mere relations a thing cannot be known in itself." The external sense gives us, therefore, "only the relation of an object to the subject, but not the inward essence (*das Innere*) which belongs to the object in itself."—Werke, iii. 72, 73, 76.

A few passages may be quoted from Hamilton, as an example of many more, in which he lays down a similar position. In the opening of his celebrated article on the Philosophy of the Conditioned, he refers to Kant's recognition of "the important principle" that "pure reason, as purely subjective, and conscious of nothing but itself," is "unable to evince the reality of aught beyond the phenomena of its personal modifications."

Again, in the same article, speaking in his own person, he says:—

"Our knowledge, whether of mind or matter, can be nothing more than a knowledge of the relative manifestations of an existence, which in itself it is our highest wisdom to recognise as beyond the reach of philosophy."—Discussions, p. 14.

"That all knowledge consists in a certain relation of the object known to the subject knowing, is self-evident. . . . All qualities both of mind and of matter are, therefore, only known to us as relations; we know nothing in itself."—Reid's Works, p. 965.

The same thought is more elaborately expressed in a well-known passage:—

"Our whole knowledge of mind and of matter is relative — conditioned — relatively conditioned. Of things absolutely or in themselves, be they external, be they internal, we know nothing, or know them only as incognisable; and become aware of their incomprehensible existence only as this is indirectly and accidentally revealed to us through certain qualities related to our faculties of knowledge. . . . All that we know is, therefore, phenomenal—phenomenal of the unknown. The philosopher, speculating the worlds of matter and of mind, is thus, in a certain sort, only an ignorant admirer. In his contemplation of the universe, the philosopher, indeed, resembles Æneas contemplating the adumbrations on his shield; as it may equally be said of the sage and the hero—

'Miraturque; rerumque ignarus, imagine gaudet.'"
—Discussions, p. 608.

"We may suppose existence to have a thousand modes; but these thousand modes are all to us as zero, unless we possess faculties accommodated to their apprehension. But were the number of our faculties coextensive with the modes of being—had we for each of these thousand modes a separate organ competent to make it known to us—still would our whole knowledge be, as it is at present, only of the relative. Of existence absolutely and in itself, we should then be as ignorant as we are now."—Metaphysics, i. 153.

The Relativistic argument thus exemplified appears to me to combine several lines of thought, from each of which it derives a certain degree of plausibility. The *first* line of thought makes the argument applicable only to the human faculties of knowledge—to man as a finite being, furnished with a certain finite apparatus for the acquisition of knowledge. The argument from the limited number of our senses lies on the surface, and Hamilton borrows it from Voltaire's philosophical apologue. With, at present, five or six avenues of knowledge, it is argued, we apprehend, as it were, only so many facets or aspects of existence. But we can conceive the number of the senses indefinitely increased—in which case each new sense would be to us the revelation of a hitherto unknown side of existence. Reality may be raying out its splendours in countless to us unknown ways, our eyes being holden meanwhile, that we cannot see. In dealing with this mode of argument, it may be readily granted that the conception is an admissible one. It may well be that the revelation of the qualities of existence which we enjoy is not complete; it may be more complete in other beings, or it may be destined to become more complete in our own case by-and-by. But it has to be noted, *first*, that this possible limitedness of our apprehension in no way discredits our actual apprehension of the qualities of the real, so far as that apprehension goes. *Secondly*, it has to be observed that such a way of speaking is fundamentally misleading, in so far as it mentions only knowledge got by the special senses, and leaves entirely out of view what Aristotle called the common sensibles. In other words, our knowledge is treated as if it were a mere mechanical ranging side by side of the data of the different senses; reason in sense is completely ignored. But we have seen in these lectures, almost to superfluity, that perception is not sensation, even from any conceivable number of senses, but that it is the presence and operation of reason in sense that constitutes knowledge of reality, even the most meagre.

This is the true retort to those also who, without enlarging on the *numerical paucity* of our avenues of knowledge, insist upon their *peculiar* character. Man, it is said, naturally swears by the truth of his own faculties; but he is evidently not a judge in the matter, for he has no other means of acquiring information. A creature with different faculties would have the same implicit confidence in the record of its faculties. Should the two ever come face to face, and begin to champion their respective faculties, who, it is asked, would be able to decide between such disputants? They apprehend reality, as it were, from different angles; what each apprehends is the truth for him—the only truth he can attain to. But who will say that either of them is in possession of the absolute truth—the absolute nature of the fact? Who will be presumptuous enough to assert that his own angle is the prescriptive angle of absolute truth? An added plausibility is sometimes lent to such arguments by giving them a physiological turn, and pointing in evidence to the varying structure of the sense-organs in different creatures. Can we suppose, it is said, that the image of the world which these different creatures form is the same for all, or must we not rather hold it to vary with the varying structure of the organs? But if this is so, who shall decide which is the absolute or normal perception? Now, as before, we need not deny a certain range of applicability to this supposition, so far as regards the data of the special senses—the so-called secondary qualities. An eye may be organised, for example, so as not to be cognisant of all the colours of the spectrum. If the eye is coarsely organised, certain of the distinctions may escape discrimination; or, its fineness being retained within certain limits, the spectrum might be shortened for it at one end or at both ends. So much we need have no hesitation in admitting. But, when generalised so as to cover the whole process of perception, the argument rests once more upon the unwarranted isolation of the senses. According to Plato's ever-fresh analogy, we must beware of supposing that we are Trojan horses, in which are perched a certain number of unconnected senses, and that the nature of knowledge may be determined by an inspection of the inlets. Impressions of sense are not knowledge; knowledge lies, as Plato says, only in the action of reason upon such impressions—ἐν δὲ τῷ περὶ ἐκείνων συλλογισμῷ. Or in our Scottish way of putting it, which is also Kant's, perception is perception by the presence of elements which could not possibly be conveyed in by any or all of the special senses. And as it is in these elements—notably in the perception of bodies as extended and as causally connected with one another—that we hold our knowledge of the world to consist, the character of such knowledge is not affected by any arguments which apply, at most, to the senses as senses.

But the issue may be accepted by the Relativist in the form in which it has now been put. When we talk of reason, it may be said, and of principles involved in perception as such, we are still confined within the circle of our own constitution. What is reason or our rational nature but a sort of psychical organisation, which may be peculiar to us as men, and may distort or modify the nature of the real in many a way, which it is, of course, impossible for us either to know or to rectify. Our pure percepts of space and time and our categories, objectifying as their influence is upon sense, may yet be merely subjective forms, and may hide from us the real nature of things, instead of revealing it. Our knowledge would then be relative only to ourselves; it would be a phenomenal knowledge—a knowledge not of things as they are, but as they appear to us. In other words, we should perceive to a great extent, if not altogether, not the actual nature of things, but just what we put into them. This, as we have seen, is the position taken up by Kant; and he was led to it by his idea that what is not given by sense must be given by the subject. What is referred to the subject passes too easily into a faculty which has to be applied to an alien or independent matter. The faculty is then represented as imposing its own constitution upon the foreign matter, and thus compelling it into moulds, which, it may be, are in no way natural to the matter itself. Scottish philosophy was fortunate enough, it seems to me, to escape this danger, by taking up the broad position that, while the principles in question are referable to the constitution of our nature, our nature is, in respect of them, in complete harmony with the nature of things—so that they may, with equal truth, be spoken of as perceived or recognised in things. A little reflection will perhaps convince us that this is the sounder and more catholic position. For, it may be asked to begin with, where does Kant derive the warrant for his *only* or *merely*, when he asserts dogmatically, as he frequently seems to do, that the forms of space and time (to go no further) are merely forms of our intuition, and have no applicability to things in themselves? He was at most entitled to put the case problematically. It is always possible that our forms of perception *may* be peculiar to ourselves, and *may* not represent the actual state of things. But it is at least equally possible that the account they give is perfectly accurate, or, in other words, that we do perceive things as they are. At least equally possible, I have said; but, in truth, what grounds of any sort exist for the supposition of distortion? I assume, of course, that the knowledge of the actual constitution of things is a desideratum; it is what we set out to know. But when we have performed the process—when we do know things in the only way possible to us — the Relativist steps in and tells us that we are not a step nearer true knowledge than before. We have falsified our own operation, and that in an inevitable and irremediable way. The mechanism of our mental constitution is expressly devised to throw us out, and to cut us off from a knowledge of things as they really are. Is this, I will simply ask, an account which commends itself to a reasonable being? Does it seem likely that everything should be expressly arranged for failure in this fashion? Surely the presumption, at all events, is all the other way. It may be granted that the abstract doubt is possible, for we see that it has been raised. It is possible that, when we have sated ourselves with knowledge, we ought always to add that, in all probability, the real things are quite different, or, at any rate, that they may be so, for all that we can know to the contrary. If any one finds ease to his conscience in the making of such provisos, I should be sorry to interfere with the satisfaction of a scrupulous nature. Again I admit that his abstract doubt can never be disproved; but, having said that, I will merely add that, for my own part, I am content to believe that no such pitfalls are laid for us. In the words of a recent writer: "We are entitled to start with the *assumption* of a harmony between the conscious and the non-conscious, perfect equivalence between the idea and the ideatum. . . . Given an external object, that object *becomes* to my consciousness. Why should the process vitiate itself? The *onus probandi* lies on him who supposes it does."[1]

But, *secondly*, the Agnostic position may be defended by placing it on a broader basis. The reference to the human faculties, as in some way possibly special in their nature, may be dropped; and the relative or merely phenomenal character of knowledge may be deduced from the consideration that knowledge is essentially and inevitably a relation. It can contain, therefore, as Kant says, "only the relation of the object to the subject, but not the inward essence which belongs to the object in itself." Kant takes up this ground in many passages, and so does Hamilton, very explicitly. "That all knowledge," says Hamilton, " consists in a certain relation of the object known to the subject knowing is self-evident. . . . All qualities both of mind and of matter are therefore only known to us as relations; we know nothing in itself." Nor could any remedy be

[1] Metaphysica Nova et Vetusta, by Scotus Novanticus, p. 45. Since these Lectures were delivered, Scotus Novanticus has laid aside his anonymity, and appeared in his own person as Professor S. S. Laurie.

found in the multiplication of our faculties or in any change wrought upon them. According to the passage already quoted: "Were the number of our faculties coextensive with the modes of being, . . . still would our knowledge be, as it is at present, only of the relative. Of existence absolutely and in itself we should then be as ignorant as we are now." In other words, to put the case quite plainly, we are necessarily cut off from knowing the real constitution of anything, because any intelligence can know only by means of its faculties of knowing. In order to know what things are, *we must know them*. But, in becoming known, the things we want to know are transformed under our hands. They are submitted to a relation in which they did not stand before; and thus we never arrive at a knowledge of the pure nature of the object—the thing in itself apart from that relation. The thing we wanted to know has escaped us, and something else lies in our grasp instead. The thing-in-itself is thus unknowable by intelligence on any terms; it must lurk in some recess of the universe unknown and unknowable even by a Divine Intelligence. For divine intelligence itself cannot know without knowing. It can only know by means of its powers of knowing, and its knowledge will be a relationing. In short, according to this account, the process of knowledge is everywhere constituted so as eternally to defeat its own end. The defect is inherent in the act as such; just because we *know* things, we are shut out from knowing the *real* things. Does not the whole position seem passing into the region of absurdity? A scathing criticism of the conception may be found in the second part of Dr Stirling's 'As regards Protoplasm.' The conclusion of the whole matter is, as Dr Stirling roundly states it, that "there is no such thing anywhere as this in-itself that is said to be unknown." We have been in pursuit of a phantom of our own creating —a shadow of the real world projected by an imperfect logic. The phantom dissolves into sheer contradiction and absurdity, as soon as we realise the full meaning and scope of the assertions that are made about it. As Ferrier puts it, "there can be an ignorance only of that of which there can be a knowledge." That which is absolutely and necessarily unknowable to all intelligence is not a name for a hidden reality, far less the type of all reality; it is simply another name for a contradiction, for nonsense.[1]

The doctrine of relativity is thus a condem-

[1] Cf. Institutes of Metaphysic, Part ii. prop. 3, and *passim*.

nation of our knowledge, and of knowledge in general, because it fails to achieve an impossibility. The untenable nature of the doctrine is probably best seen when it is contemplated in its generality, as has just been done. But the widespread acceptance which, in one form or another, it enjoys, is probably due to the existence of certain correlative notions which we are continually employing in experience, and which lend themselves readily to misuse. The notions in question are such as substance and quality, noumenon and phenomenon, the thing-in-itself and its appearance, the essence and its manifestation, the Ego and its actions or states. Correlative notions or conceptions are conceptions each of which exists only through the other; and where there is nothing expressed but the pure fact of correlation, we may go further, and say with truth that the one correlative actually *is* the other. But, just because this is so, it is only necessary to separate these inseparables, in order to arrive at the conclusion that one of them is either non-existent, or, as is contended by the thinkers we are dealing with, unknowable. The familiar conjunction of substance and quality is suddenly transformed into the grandiose opposition of the Unknowable and its manifestation. All that we have to do is to apply the logic of abstract identity, which asserts that a thing is eternally itself, and not another thing. The qualities are the qualities, and the substance is the substance; the substance is, accordingly, different from the qualities. We may know the qualities; but it does not therefore follow that, in the qualities, we know the substance. On the contrary, it follows, as we have no extra-knowledge to show, that our knowledge is limited to the qualities or the phenomenal, while substance or the noumenon lurks behind unknown. Hamilton accepts this position in the fullest sense. "There are two opposite series of expressions," he says: "first, those which denote the relative and the known; and secondly, those which denote the absolute and the unknown. Of the former class are the words phenomenon, mode, modification, state. Of the latter class—that is, the absolute and the unknown—is the word subject, and its analogous expressions, substance and sub-stratum."[1] Thus "mind and matter, as known or knowable, are only two different series of phenomena or qualities; mind and matter, as unknown and unknowable, are the two substances in which these two

[1] Lectures on Metaphysics, i. 148.

different series of phenomena or qualities are supposed to inhere."[1] This line of thought (which may perhaps be called a *third* thread in the relativist argument) conducts Hamilton, as it had conducted Kant before him, to the assertion that we are ignorant not only of the real nature of things, but also of the real nature of our own selves. This conclusion might excusably be treated as a *reductio ad absurdum* of the doctrine, and of the logic which leads to it; but the doctrine has found favour with so many eminent philosophers, that it demands a fuller and more respectful consideration. It is not altogether easy, however, to discover what these philosophers, who dilate upon our ignorance of substance, would consider to be a knowledge of substance. On the one hand, they seem to fall back into the line of thought already exposed, which virtually challenges us to know without knowing—to take hold of a thing without touching it. On the other hand, it seems as if they insisted on knowing substance, not as we actually do know it, but by sense—that is, as a separate sensation added at the end of the series or complex of sensations which constitute its qualities. The truth is, on the contrary, that qualities as

[1] Lectures on Metaphysics, i. 138.

qualities are no more given by sense than substance is. The correlative conceptions are given together, being apprehended by reason, and necessarily employed by reason for the understanding of the object before it. Their use is to make the object intelligible, not to mystify the observer by surreptitiously doubling the object before his eyes; and the ordinary man, it may be added, is fully satisfied that he does understand by their means. Yet the question has proved a veritable Serbonian bog, in which whole armies of philosophers have sunk; and the unknowableness of substance may justly be said to have become a philosophic superstition. Berkeley's delicate irony hits off the situation better than any words of mine could do. "'We are miserably bantered,' say philosophers, 'by our senses, and amused only with the outside and show of things. The real essence—the internal qualities and constitution—of every, the meanest, object is hid from our view; something there is in every drop of water, every grain of sand, which it is beyond the power of human understanding to fathom or comprehend.'"[1] It is to this idea of an essence, distinct from the qualities, and to be known, if known at all, alongside of the qualities,

[1] Principles of Human Knowledge, section 101.

that philosophers are indebted, he says, "for being ignorant of what everybody else knows perfectly well."[1]

If we go to the root of the matter, I think it will be found that the misconception is due to the influence of a false logic—of what I have called the logic of abstract identity. Though it is not too much to say that this logic is refuted by the whole structure of nature and of reason, it appears to be exceedingly difficult for the human mind to emancipate itself from its trammels. To be sure, there is identity in things, but it is an identity in difference. Identity is only asserted because of difference, and is only cognisable through difference. Difference is stamped everywhere upon nature and upon thought; without it predication would become at once impossible. An affirmative judgment is the assertion of an identity in difference; a negative judgment asserts

---

[1] See the opening of the Third Dialogue between Hylas and Philonous. People speak, he says elsewhere, as if "we might know our soul as we know a triangle" (Principles, § 136). Berkeley's own view of material substance would have been more satisfactory, if he had extended to it the principle which he here applies to the mind or the subject of thought; for the argument proceeds *pari passu* in the two cases. But however that may be, his impeachment of the bastard mysticism of the relativists is as sound and trenchant still as upon the day it was written.

a difference in an underlying identity. The very form of the judgment distinguishes subject and predicate while it unites them. The calling of a thing by its name carries with it the same implication; for names are general terms or universals, and they express certain qualities of the object—certain points of community, that is, with different objects. Were it not that the object does possess qualities,—that it exists, in short, as a living refutation of the doctrine of abstract identity,—it would be impossible to employ a name in its regard. Of course we all know that a name may be given, at first, to a single object, and only afterwards extended by analogy to other objects that resemble the first in certain respects. But, from the moment of its first imposition upon that one object, it is, in Mill's language, potentially the name of a class; it is from the first a general term—a universal—though it may chance to be applied only to one individual. In a word, the name is not applied to the individual, considered as an abstract point of unity which is nothing but its own undifferentiated self—a mere " one " or " this " in the presence of countless similarly self-identical " ones " or " thises." It is applied to the individual, as the ordinary logic books tell us, to express certain prominent or striking aspects, henceforth called attributes or qualities, of the individual. And accordingly—just because it is not a mark put upon a mere particular—it is from the beginning capable of extension to other individuals, which are found to possess the same qualities. It is sometimes said, as by Locke for instance, that general names are needed in order "to abridge discourse," seeing that it is "beyond the power of human capacity to frame and retain distinct ideas of all the particular things we meet with."[1] Now it is so far from being true that general names or universals are only makeshifts for an infinite number of proper names, that even the possession of an infinite store of such names would not enable us to think one jot, or to frame a single sentence. Each object being a mere particular, an existential point, no occasion for predication could arise; for, at the most, we could but say of each that it was itself—that A was A. But, in such a world, this proposition would be "trifling" indeed, and the very form of predication or judgment would be absent. We cannot predicate substances of one another, and there would be no adjectives. The infinite number of proper names would be like so many unmeaning numerical marks put upon absolutely non-resem-

[1] Essay, iii. 3, 2.

bling objects. We cannot say of five that it is six, or of any one number that it is another number.

Thus it is that extreme Nominalism refutes itself, as is well seen in the Nominalists of antiquity who are brought before us in Plato's 'Theætetus' and elsewhere. These Cynic Nominalists had the courage of their opinions, and dialectic skill enough to perceive the legitimate conclusions from their principles. They did not hesitate, therefore, to maintain that every combination of subject and predicate is impossible, since the conception of the one is different from the conception of the other, and two things thus different can never be declared to be the same. Definition they maintained to be impossible, for all that is real is particular, and can only be explained by the utterance of its proper name. But we have seen that, on the contrary, the particular as particular—the mere self-identical unqualified particular—nowhere exists; it is the abstraction of a logic not wholly clear about its own procedure. And the thing-in-itself is simply the fallacy of the mere particular in another form. The mere particular and the mere universal are alike abstractions of the mind; what exists is *the individual*. All that is real is—not particular but —individual; and the individual is a particular that is also universal, or, from the other side, it is a universal—a set of universals—particularised. Individuality consists, as Bain expresses it, in "a conflux of generalities." The two sides are always there, and each is only through the other. There is no existence which is not determined so-and-so—that is, there is no substance without qualities; and equally there are no qualities without a substance to which they are referred. It is the nature of reality so to be, and it is the nature of thought so to think. But the substance is not an existence distinct from the qualities—something that can be separated from the qualities and known by itself. The substance exists as qualified, and we know it through its qualities. How else should we know it? The idea of an existence in each thing, beyond the existence which we know and name; a substance in itself that shall not be known through its qualities; a cause that has no necessary reference to its effect; a man that shall not be known by his thoughts and actions; a God that shall be concealed by his own manifestation,—such is the idea that underlies all varieties of Agnosticism; and in truth it is one of the most curious delusions that ever possessed the mind of man.

Yet it is an idea so common at the present day

as almost to have passed into the structure of language. The very function of the phenomenon would seem to be to expound, express, manifest, or reveal the noumenon; but the exact contrary is implied in the current use of the terms. It is hardly possible to open a scientific or semi-philosophical work, without meeting the complacent admission that our knowledge is "only of phenomena." Or the writer tells us that the science in question, so far as he is concerned, treats only of phenomena, the consideration of the corresponding noumena being relegated to philosophy or metaphysics. It is true the time never comes for the metaphysical investigation which is thus held over; and the statement is doubtless often made as a kind of polite conciliation to the "metaphysicians" who still linger in our midst. Those who make it have a shrewd suspicion that noumena are things a sensible man need never have anything to do with, and that the science which professes to deal with them is pretty nigh exploded. And so metaphysics well might be, if it were really the science of noumena, as these men understand noumena. But they may rest assured that the best result of this contemned metaphysics in modern times has been just this—to explode the conception of such duplicate entities as they still cannot help half believing in, and to repudiate, in consequence, the brand of that "only" before phenomena. Certainly the objects of our knowledge are phenomena; for phenomenon is the name we give to an object in relation to our knowledge of it. But, in knowing the phenomenon, we know the object itself through and through—so far, of course, as we do know it, so far as it has really become a phenomenon for us. In short, to say that we know phenomena is only to say twice over that we know; to say that the noumenon becomes a phenomenon is only to say that the noumenon is known.

It is true that we do not know the *whole* nature, probably, of anything; and the term noumenon is useful, therefore, as contrasting the object, in all the completeness of the qualities which really belong to it, with the comparatively imperfect knowledge of its qualities which we have yet attained. The noumenon is the object from the point of view of the universe; the phenomenon is the same object from the point of view of human knowledge. The noumenon embraces, in this way, the qualities yet to be discovered as well as those already known; while the term phenomenon is necessarily limited to what we actually know. But if, *ex hypothesi*, a thing were completely to phenomenalise itself to us—*i.e.*, if we had an exhaustive knowledge of the qualities of any single thing—then the knowledge of the phenomenon would be, in that case, in the strictest sense the knowledge of the noumenon. The noumenon is nothing but the manifold and different qualities reflected into unity. Qualities do not fly loose, and afterwards get "collected"; they cannot be known otherwise than as unified and centred in a thing. You have never, in short, either bare subjects or bare attributes, but always attributes referred to subjects, always subjects clothed with attributes—that is, always identity through difference, and difference subsumed into identity.

It is perfectly evident that the line of thought which separates the noumenon from the phenomenon must inevitably end in the assertion of an Unknown and Unknowable as the ultimate reality of the universe. For, as we have seen, there *is* nothing to know in the noumenon, if it be separated from the phenomenon. It is simply an abstraction which we have converted into a fetish. Kant and Hamilton are, accordingly, the fathers of all such, in modern times, as traffic in the Unknowable. The 'Critique' denies us all knowledge of reality, whether of the world, of

Self, or of God; and Hamilton tells us the same thing again and again. He has already been quoted on our ignorance both of mind and matter; and I need do no more than recall his favourite utterances in regard to the Unknown God. "The last and highest consecration of all true religion must be an altar—ἀγνώστῳ θεῷ—'To the unknown and unknowable God.'" A learned ignorance, he tells us, is the consummation of knowledge.[1] To be sure, both Kant and Hamilton profess to repair the breaches of their knowledge by the aid of Faith or Belief. Kant represents his whole industry in the speculative sphere as undertaken in the interests of a moral faith. In his own words, he abolishes knowledge to make room for belief. The Practical Reason is to heal the wounds inflicted by the Speculative; and the first 'Critique' is accordingly only a necessary negative preliminary to the second.[2] In like manner, Hamilton is reproached by Mill with bringing back under the name of Belief the very things he had rejected as Knowledge. "When I deny that the Infinite can by us be *known*," writes Hamilton, "I am far from

---

[1] Cf. Discussions, pp. 15, 36.
[2] See the preface to the second edition of the Critique of Pure Reason.

denying that by us it is, must, and ought to be *believed*. This I have indeed anxiously evinced, both by reasoning and authority."[1] This is, indeed, the very purport of the Philosophy of the Conditioned. Of the contradictories, which are both inconceivable, one must nevertheless be true—*i.e.*, must be believed in as existing. The "learned ignorance" which is "the end of philosophy," is declared in one place to be "the beginning of theology."[2] The philosophy of the Conditioned, he says again, "is professedly a scientific demonstration of the impossibility of that 'wisdom in high matters' which the Apostle prohibits us even to attempt; and it proposes, from the limitation of the human powers, from our impotence to comprehend what, however, we must admit, to show articulately why the secret things of God cannot but be to man past finding out."[3]

We know how this was developed in a theological reference by Mansel in his famous Bampton Lectures on the Limits of Religious Thought. "In the impotence of reason," as he says in his 'Metaphysics,' "we are compelled to take refuge in faith." Hence reason has to be shown to be impotent, in order to make room for faith. Time

[1] Lectures on Metaphysics, ii. 530.   [2] Ibid., i. 34.
[3] Discussions, p. 598.

may perhaps be said to have already pronounced upon this new presentation of a well-worn argument; and it is perhaps not necessary now to do more than allude to the equivocal character of the position. Reason has often enough been abased, in order that Faith might be exalted; but only too frequently there is the ring of insincerity in the voice that pleads. It insinuates an inference which it does not draw. In Hamilton and Mansel, of course, there is no suspicion of such disingenuous dealing; yet the whole argument is like playing with edged tools. If the inventors of the tools remain unharmed, the next to handle them will surely cut their fingers. When reason is sapped, we may depend upon it that, in the long-run, men will pass over, not to theological faith, but to complete Agnosticism. We see this exemplified for us by the actual course of events. We see Kant's deductions from the practical reason entirely disregarded by the vast majority of those who invoke his name. Kant is, as has been said, the *fons et origo* of the most cultured Agnosticism of the day. His negative criticism has lived; his positive reconstruction is, for the majority, as if it had never been. And as for Hamilton, Hamilton's arguments stand in the forefront of Herbert Spencer's 'First Principles.'

These examples should be enough to prove the treacherous nature of any argument which bases religion upon ignorance. The faith bred of ignorance is neither stable nor is it likely to be enlightened. It will either be a completely empty acknowledgment, as we see in the belief in the Unknowable, or it will be an arbitrary play of poetic fancy, such as is proposed by Lange for our consolation. Our phenomenal world, says Lange, is a world of materialism; but still the Beyond of the Unknowable remains to us. There we may figure to ourselves an ampler and diviner air, and may construct a more perfect justness and goodness than we find upon earth. The poets—in word and music and painting—are the chief interpreters of this land of the Ideal. To them we must go, if we would restore our jaded spirits. But we may not ask — or if we do, we cannot learn — whether this fairy-land exists, or whether it has any relation to the world of fact. To all which it may be confidently replied, that such an empty play of fancy can discharge the functions neither of philosophy nor of religion. The synthesis of philosophy and the clear confidence of religion may both, in a sense, transcend the actual data before us, and may both, therefore, have a certain affinity with poetry; but the synthesis is valueless and the confidence ill-based if they do not express our deepest insight into facts, and our deepest belief as to the ultimate nature of things. Religion, therefore, if it is to retain the place which it has always held in human life and thought, must be based on reason, as it has been based heretofore by all the great philosophic doctors and the masters of theology. It must be shown to be our reasonable service.

In all this, Hamilton and Mansel must be held, I think, to depart from the catholic doctrine and traditional tendency of Scottish philosophy, as observable before their time and since. Reid expresses his repugnance to such a mode of argument, in words which might almost have been written in view of the subsequent development. "Some good men," he says, "have been led to depreciate the human understanding, and to put out the light of nature and reason, in order to exalt that of revelation. Those weapons which were taken up in support of religion, are now employed to overturn it; and what was by some accounted the bulwark of orthodoxy, is become the stronghold of atheism and infidelity. Atheists . . . join hands with theologians in depreciating the human understanding, that they may lead us into absolute scepticism."[1] And with special applicability to Mansel's depreciation of the moral or practical reason, he says in another place: "If moral judgment be a true and real judgment, the principles of morals stand upon the immutable foundation of truth, and can undergo no change by any difference of fabric or structure of those who judge of them. There may be, and there are, beings who have not the faculty of conceiving moral truths, or perceiving the excellence of moral worth [as there are beings incapable of perceiving the truths of mathematics]; but no defect, no error of understanding, can make what is true to be false."[2]

In spite of these brave words, however, the little rift within the lute may be detected even in Reid. It lurks wherever the metaphysic of substance and quality is imperfectly or carelessly apprehended. There are not more than one or two passages in Reid which could be fixed upon a Relativist; but one of them is so explicit as to be sufficient. "By the mind of man," it is said, "we understand that in him which thinks, remembers, reasons, wills. The essence both of body and of mind is unknown to us. We know

[1] Works, p. 636.     [2] Ibid., p. 679.

certain properties of the first and certain operations of the last, and by these only we can define or describe them."[1] But as there is nowhere any further reference to this unknown entity, and as the argument is nowhere coloured by its existence, the statement here sounds in Reid almost like an echo—an echo perhaps from his studies of Locke—a current phrase accepted without much thought. At all events, it is certain that the doctrine is in no way peculiar to Reid or prominent in his system; there is not a word of Phenomenalism or Agnosticism throughout his writings. It may be said that, at one point, he directly asserts that we have only relative notions of body and mind. But when he goes on to explain himself, he turns out to mean no more than that our "notion of body is not direct, but *relative to its qualities*. We know that it is something extended, solid, and divisible, but we know no more." Similarly our notion of mind is "relative to its operations."[2] That is, neither is known by immediate presentation in sense or in internal consciousness, but both are known *through* these presentations, and only in relation to them. In itself, this statement is quite consistent with the doctrine laid down in this Lecture; and if Reid meant no more than

[1] Works, p. 220.     [2] Ibid., p. 513.

this by his previous assertion about the essence of body and mind, the phrase would be shorn of its dangers. Taken together, however, we may probably admit that the two passages do insinuate an unknown existence behind, though Reid evidently had not thought out the question for himself. But when we come to Dugald Stewart, we have the Hamiltonian theory already pretty definitely foreshadowed. Stewart expressly asserts the knowledge of qualities and the accompanying ignorance of substance, and bases philosophical arguments upon the position.[1] As Dr M'Cosh points out, it only remained for Hamilton to connect the qualitative theory of Stewart with the phenomenal theory of Kant. But it is doubtless true, as the same writer maintains,[2] that Stewart himself would not have accepted the identification. At all events, he was not aware of what was afterwards to be deduced from his theory, or grafted upon it. As soon as Hamilton and Mansel had brought full-blown relativity to light, the instinct of the school shrank back from such conclusions; and Scottish philosophers set about a more careful revision of their premisses.

[1] Cf. the opening chapter of the Outlines of the Philosophy of the Human Mind.
[2] Scottish Philosophy, p. 289.

Even Mansel receded from the Kantio-Hamiltonian doctrine of a merely phenomenal knowledge of Self; and the most typical writers of the school have only been driven by the Kantian doctrine into a clearer assertion of our direct knowledge of reality. In this respect, the true tradition of the school is upheld by writers like Professor Calderwood, Professor Flint, and Dr M'Cosh of Princeton, in each of whom, I think, we may trace the same reaction against Relativism. Differing widely from Hegel in many respects, such Scottish thinkers are at one with him in their repudiation of the Phenomenalistic doctrine which has been examined in the present lecture. To me it seems that, whatever we may think of the Hegelian system in other respects, we have here one great gift which it has bestowed on the world — the insight into the logic of this pervasive fallacy. So far as I can see, Hegel alone of all metaphysicians lifts us completely clear of Relativism. He alone has gone systematically to work to lay bare the abstractions on which it depends; and, in so doing, he has to a great extent transformed the character of metaphysics, and so rendered unjust many of the epithets which popular phraseology still associates with the science.

# LECTURE VI.

### THE POSSIBILITY OF PHILOSOPHY AS SYSTEM:
### SCOTTISH PHILOSOPHY AND HEGEL.

OUR position being thus defined in reference to Relativism and Agnosticism, there remains the important question of the relation of Scottish philosophy, or at least of what we hold to be the legitimate outcome of Scottish philosophy, to what has been called by Professor Fraser "Gnosticism"—*i.e.*, to philosophy as a closed circle or completed system, in some such form as it is presented, for example, by Hegel. If we repudiate Relativism, are we prepared to be called Absolutists?

A question, similar in its terms, was essayed by Hamilton in his celebrated article on the Philosophy of the Conditioned, and in his repeated attacks upon the doctrines of the Absolute. I do not propose to traverse once more that deserted field of battle; but as the very term Absolute associates itself to Scottish ears with Hamilton, a few words of explanation may serve to remove misapprehensions. In regard to this particular controversy, time has brought us nearer to the Continent than we were in the beginning of the century, and has enabled us to see that, in the case of Hegel at least, the issue raised by Sir W. Hamilton is an entirely false one. The point which Hamilton makes, Hegel would be the last man in the world to deny. The Absolute, whose unknowableness Hamilton maintains, is, in his own words, a thing existing "not under relation"—"the absolute negation of all relation." It is "absolutely one," and "absolute unity is convertible with the absolute negation of plurality and difference." Hence "intelligence whose essence is plurality—the plurality of subject and object—cannot be identified with the Absolute."[1] In other words, the Absolute against which Hamilton contends is precisely the abstraction of a wholly relationless thing-in-itself which we have demolished—the very abstraction against which we find Hegel inveighing at every turn. Hegel's system, indeed, may not inaptly be styled

[1] Cf. Discussions, pp. 32, 33.

the reasoned refutation of this delusive abstraction. The real difference between Hegel and Hamilton is that Hamilton, blinded by his doctrine of Relativity, still believes in the existence of what is demonstrably unknowable; while Hegel holds it to be at once unknowable and non-existent. And Intelligence, which, on account of its inherent difference, is pronounced by Hamilton incompetent to his own abstract Absolute, *is itself* Hegel's Absolute. Intelligence *qua* intelligence, knowledge *qua* knowledge, is, so to speak, a transparent relation — a relation in which, as Aristotle long ago said, the two sides are one. It is a relation, therefore, in which a real identity is reached through plurality or difference. In the act of knowledge, so far forth as there is perfect knowledge, the difference of subject and object is, in the current phrase, transcended or overcome. But this does not mean that it disappears, and that the two sides fall together in a blank or pure identity. Pure identity—Hamilton's Absolute—is coma or annihilation.

And this is what we find too in Mysticism, for example, when it runs itself out to its legitimate conclusion. Mysticism is, in great part, a blind revolt against the fact of difference, the fact of relatedness, which meets us inevitably in every instance of knowledge. It is the logic of identity applied in religion. The mystic pines for the abolition of all distinction between himself and the object of his desire. It is a mood more or less natural to us all. The fact of relation seems to bring separation with it; it seems to cleave existence as by a sheer chasm, and to cut us off from perfect union with God, as well as from communion with the vast inarticulate life of nature in which we are rooted. Who has not felt the sense of strangeness and deep longing in his heart, on the hillside or in the glen, perhaps, on a sweet day of spring — deep tear-begetting longing toward the ancestral mother—longing, as it were, to burst our individual bounds, and close with "all we flow from, soul in soul"? But in truth we know not what we ask in such moments of dim craving in the blood. To be made one with nature would be to resign our knowledge and our consciousness, to merge in the dumb being of natural forces, to be no more as we have been, and to lose, therefore, the very penetrative sense of life and enjoyment that prompts the desire. In like manner, the religious feeling overleaps itself in its desire for closer union with God — the object of its intensest aspiration and love. Knowledge seems to divide while it unites; it seems, therefore, as if knowledge must be transcended and left behind, if supreme communion is to be attained. Hence the hungering and thirsting of men's hearts after some immediate perception or intuition of the Godhead — some supra-intellectual union, nay, contact or fusion with the source of all. But such fusing of the skirts of self is not rising but sinking in the scale of existence. The abnegation of Self is the abnegation of intelligence and consciousness, for which it substitutes either a total blank, or, at most, a state resembling the dull sensation of the lowest organism. It is a curious irony of logic which leads those who would most highly exalt the divine to degrade it so low. But if we object to relation, and do away with difference, this is the goal at which we must ultimately arrive. If God is to be God in any real sense, His life cannot be the pulseless identity of a Spinozistic substance, but must realise itself in such a "kingdom of grace" as Leibnitz spoke of—a divine polity of spirits, each of whom intelligence, infinitely dividing and infinitely uniting, raises into a fresh image of God, a new focus of the life of things.

Intelligence, then, bears difference eternally in its heart. Thereby alone does it exist as intelligence. We need, therefore, follow out this argument about the Absolute no further upon the Hamiltonian track. Hamilton's Absolute is not asserted by Hegel, and the existence of Hegel's Absolute—that is, of the fact which Hegel names the Absolute—cannot be denied by Hamilton. What has been said so far, has been said only to guard against possible misconception, and against the possible accusation of neglect; and we have seen that Hamilton's discussion only serves to confuse the issues. This, unfortunately, must be our verdict upon great part of those speculations which were most distinctively Hamilton's own. Reasons have been adduced to show that they are no genuine development of Scottish philosophy; and what Hamilton adopted from Kant consisted of the most questionable parts of that philosopher's theory. He nowhere brings us into contact with the full doctrine of Kant; and his refutation of Hegel, by proving against Hegel the very thing that Hegel himself insisted on, is a specimen of misrepresentation that hardly admits of excuse. Hamilton had a great personal influence, and, by his marvellous erudition and his great powers of mind, he dignified the study of philosophy in these islands. He may almost be said to have lifted it to a higher plane. By his constant references to the great German thinkers he excited curiosity, and, as it were, brought our island philosophy into contact with the philosophy of the Continent—a contact which was destined to bear much fruit at a later date, as the distinctive tenets of Hamiltonianism began to fall into forgetfulness. Hamilton made valuable contributions to psychology, and he also gave an impetus to the study of formal logic. On these departments of his activity, on his contributions to the literature of philosophy, and on the personal influence which he exerted upon a large number of thinkers—and not upon his properly philosophical speculations—I am persuaded that his fame will ultimately rest.

Let us avoid, then, all discussions in which the Absolute is used as equivalent to the thing-in-itself. Absolutism is the true doctrine, if by that is meant only that our knowledge, so far as it goes, is a knowledge of reality. But when the spectre of Relativity has been finally laid, the only instructive sense in which the term Absolute can be used, is as applied to the *system*. An absolute system is one which claims to *demonstrate* the rationality of existence. And the only way in which such a demonstration can be given, is by embracing all the elements of existence in the final synthesis. We must assign to all their place within the system; or, what is the same thing, we must show their relation to the harmony of the whole. The question is, therefore, Do we possess such a system? Have we this insight into the connection and harmony of the whole?

And here, at the outset, it seems desirable to say a few words upon the remarkable contrast which exists, in reference to this question, between the philosophers of this country and the philosophers of Germany—words which may be, to a certain extent, a palinode, inasmuch as they must modify in some degree the high praise that has been bestowed, and bestowed justly, on the achievement of Reid. Germany may be system-ridden; and in the old days, when every university professor was said to carry a scheme of the universe in his pocket, no doubt this system-mongering was carried to a pitch of absurdity. But, on the other hand, it is possible to imbibe a prejudice against system which may be, in the end, to the full as dangerous. We may be justly repelled by the premature syntheses and the jaunty confidence of many of these system-makers, but we ought to beware lest our reaction from their error crystallise into a settled repugnance to everything in systematic form. The natural man within us is only too ready to believe that there is no harmony discoverable in things, because we are thereby absolved from the labour of seeking it. It is important to remember that despair of system is despair of philosophy, for philosophy just *is* system. As in the old Roman days, therefore, men honoured the general, inefficient though he was, who had not despaired of the Republic, so we ought to honour the indomitable confidence in reason which continually impels men afresh to organise their knowledge and make it a whole. The spirit of philosophy lives more in such attempts than in a cherished distrust of the possibility of success. There is one doom which Plato pronounces to be the worst of all: "Let us above all things take heed," he says in the 'Phædo,' "that one misfortune does not befall us. Let us not become misologues ($\mu\iota\sigma\acute{o}\lambda o\gamma o\iota$), as some people become misanthropes; for no greater evil can befall men than to become haters of reason."

The earlier Scottish philosophers were not so much liable to this danger. Their warfare was not with the system-builder, but with the sceptic. But there can be no question that they exhibit a regrettable indifference to considerations of system and completeness. In their matter, as we might put it, they coincide, so far as they go, with Kant and Hegel; but the matter has not received at their hands the form that properly belongs to it. Their principles are not connected with one another; and they have the appearance, consequently, of hanging in the air without mutual support. They remain isolated intuitions, instead of constituting a system of principles. Reid is in the main at the Intuitional point of view, where a certain number of "loose" or isolated propositions are accepted as self-evident, and treated as principles. Kant, on the other hand, was deeply impressed with the idea of system. Though he sometimes carried it to extreme lengths, and though his own systematic principle is vitiated by the implicit trust it implies in the soundness and sufficiency of formal logic—though it exhibits ingenuity rather than far-reaching insight—yet Kant's ideal of the conceptions of reason as springing from the absolute unity of the understanding was of all-important influence upon the further development of philosophy in Germany. When we come to Hegel, we find a Method put into our hands, which professes to guarantee both the inter-connectedness of all the conceptions, and the self-completing integrity of the resulting scheme. Now, no one will deny that Hegel's analysis of the conceptions of reason as reason is the product of infinite industry, and of a metaphysical insight at once subtle and profound. It is an indefinite advance on anything that had gone before it in modern philosophy. Compared with Hegel's 'Science of Logic,' Kant's scheme of the categories is but a meagre sketch. But though we may admit all this, what are we to say of the claim to completeness, and of the dialectic method on which it is based? The answer will depend upon the meaning we put into the term method.

The Method, so far as that means an invariable self-repeating formula, has been quietly shelved of late, even by those whose thoughts have been most plainly moulded by Hegel. Evidently there is no royal road to philosophical completeness, any more than to any other result worth having. Hegel would not have spoken as he does of "the labour of the Notion," if he had had nothing to do but to *set* his apparatus at Being and Nothing, and let it unwind itself of its own accord. It is not unnatural for a man to be overridden by an important principle which he has brought to light; and Hegel is not free from this failing. But it was only, I think, with the rank and file of the Hegelian army that the dialectic method actually became a fetish. For a fetish it has become to any one who supposes that, for the final and satisfying account of any subject, a mechanical application of the formula suffices. Philosophical work cannot yet be done by machinery. A method or formula would lead to nothing but a barren repetition of itself, unless it were fed continually from the looms of fact. We have Hegel's own word for it, that the Method is nothing, unless we bring the whole nature of thought with us. The Method is no magic formula, then, and it will open no doors save in a master's hand. Yet the significance of the thought that inspires it cannot lightly be over-estimated; and we may easily do scant justice to the depth and the reach of Hegel's insight. The Method sums up a thought which may almost be said to constitute Hegel's philosophy, and one which, in my opinion, gives him a signal advantage over all his modern predecessors.

The thought in question is primarily a logical principle; a fact, which may partly explain why Hegel made his 'Logik' the centre of his system. It is the principle to which we have already referred so often, the systematic recognition of the fact that thought is founded upon difference; whereas identity had hitherto been the god of the logician's idolatry. I do not profess to follow, or even to indicate, all Hegel's applications of his principle, nor should I care to defend them all. But I do believe that here we have a principle, not of arbitrary invention, but drawn from the heart of things—from the nature of the self-conscious spirit itself. It is no unreasonable expectation, then, that a principle drawn from such a source will be found verifying itself in an infinite variety of directions. Barely logical as the principle seems, it is matter of biography that Hegel formulated it in its breadth only after the profoundest study of man and history, and, in particular, of the religious consciousness. His text, too, is being proclaimed from the house-tops to-day by those to whom his name, if known at all, is known only as a byword and a reproach. What is the biological explanation of life and the organism but a denial of dead identity? What is development but the same denial of static sameness, along with the assertion of identity in difference? But though the principle meets us everywhere, Hegel alone has been consistent in his metaphysical applications of it, and clear as to his own procedure. And it is because the principle of his Method is derived directly from the nature of self-consciousness, that Hegel's results are so marvellously richer than those of Kant. Because the direct relation of all principles of explanation to the nature of the explaining self was not adequately grasped either by Kant or Reid, their enumerations of principles have unavoidably the appearance of being, as it were, in the air. The mutual connection of the principles is not displayed, and they do not lead up, as in Hegel they necessarily do, to the central principle from which they hold their own existence in fee. I do not for a moment believe that the Method guarantees Hegel's list of the conceptions of reason to be the best possible, either in point of completeness or in point of order. The working out of such a grammar of thought is necessarily a case of progressive approximation towards an unattained ideal; and I do not think that Hegel himself contemplated any finality as regards the filling-in of his scheme. The essential point in a systematic philosophy is simply the possession of some outline or schema, by reference to which each conception may be judged, and receive its place and meaning. In Self-consciousness, Hegel seems to hold a position from which, in the nature of the case, it is impossible to dislodge him.

But there may be a misconception fostered by Hegel's way of putting things—a misconception which seems to cling persistently to all forms of Idealism. Idealism is almost invariably conceived as if it had some design upon the reality of the world. It is supposed to consist in robbing the object of its substantiality in order to enrich the subject; or, as absolute idealism, it is supposed to sap reality altogether by depriving it of its solid consistency, and reducing it to a dance of ideas or thought-relations. But we may readily believe that this cannot be any man's serious intention; and the true scope of absolute idealism is quite different. It denies reality neither in the subject nor in the object, neither here nor there. Its sole thesis is, that the real is ultimately rational—*i.e.*, that its different elements constitute a system, in which, and in which alone, they can be understood. To assert their existence outside of the system—apart from the mutual reference of each to all—is certainly, according to such a philosophy, inadmissible; but it is inadmissible, simply because it is unmeaning. Philosophy, as such, is a war against abstractions, against stopping too soon, against treating parts as wholes, against isolating things from their connections. And in this sense, absolute idealism certainly does deprive the parts of their supposed independent substantiality. But it is inexorably just in that it metes to all with the same measure;

all members of the system alike are real, but all alike hold their reality in fee from the system to which they belong. They exist as parts and not otherwise; the whole alone can be said to exist absolutely or in its own right.

But perhaps, as I have said, Hegel is himself partly to blame. His method of presentation may be partly responsible for the idea that he reduces the universe, in Mr Bradley's vivid phrase, to "an unearthly ballet of bloodless categories." It seems as if we were asked to believe that the chain of thought-determinations unfolded in the 'Logic' really *is* the life of the world—as if the reality of God and man and things veritably consisted in these abstractions. What wonder if we are told, that to offer us this organisation of thought as the ultimate account of the world is to give us a stone when we ask for bread. It is this that lends force, for example, to Lotze's strictures upon the Hegelian system. The system seems, if this be true, to eviscerate reality of all inner content, and to present us with a set of labels or formulæ instead. Or as Mr Bradley puts it, "The notion that existence could be the same as understanding, strikes as cold and ghost-like as the dreariest materialism. . . . Though dragged to such conclusions, we cannot embrace them.

Our principles may be true, but they are not reality. They no more *make* that Whole which commands our devotion, than some shredded dissection of human tatters *is* that warm and breathing beauty of flesh which our hearts found delightful."[1] But indeed, knowledge, as Fichte said, just because it is knowledge, is not reality. It is an account of reality. To speak as if the categories of the Hegelian Logic were real existences, is not less absurd than it would be to identify the planetary system with the mathematical and mechanical laws of its operation, which are contained in a text-book on Astronomy. Existence must consist in a Life of some sort, with those possibilities of feeling, of internal reflection and enjoyment, which alone, as Lotze insists, give worth or value to the universe, and make it more than a species of binomial theorem.

We may be helped here, I think, in reaching a true conclusion, by recurring to a position which we found important in the preceding lecture—the position, namely, that the real, or what actually exists, is the individual. This thesis we were there engaged in defending against the supposition of the abstract particular, the unqualified thing-in-itself. But it has equally to be defended

[1] Principles of Logic, p. 533.

against the supposition that the real can consist of abstract universals. It seems difficult to maintain the just mean between these two extremes. On the one hand, men fall into the belief that, in the heart of reality, behind all that we know of it, there lurks an unknowable kernel or substance, which, as it were, makes the qualities exist. This supposed skeleton of the world must be admitted to be, as the Hegelians contend, a *caput mortuum* or mere abstraction. It is the abstract particular, the predicateless subject, the unrelated unit. But, on the other hand, empty generals can no more exist as such than empty particulars. Predicates, unreferred to a subject, would be as bad as Hume's "entirely loose" ideas. Now Hegel's 'Logic' is a system of predicates. Accordingly the categories which he there unrolls must be regarded as descriptions of the world, not the world itself. The universe must exist as a real Being, or system of beings, whose life may be interpreted according to these logical formulæ, but is certainly not exhausted in their exemplification.

Indeed, from a logical point of view, the universe may be usefully regarded as one vast individual. Now, it is of the nature of an individual to be inexhaustible in its qualities or predicates. This is true even of a finite individual. For it may be said that, if we could thoroughly know any single thing, we should in the same act thoroughly know all things. According to the Leibnitian phrase, "eyes as piercing as those of God" would be able to read in the changes of a single monad all the changes of the universe. But when the same point of view is extended to the universe, the necessary inexhaustibleness of the individual becomes still more apparent; and this consideration may help us to a true position as between the abstract particular and the abstract universal—as between Agnosticism and Gnosticism. Our knowledge of the universe we must hold to be true and valid. So far as it goes, it expresses the actual nature of the fact, and there is nothing in the fact that is essentially unknowable. But, on the other hand, there is a great deal which is *unknown*, and which, we may predict, will always remain unknown to the finite intelligence. We know the universe truly so far as we do know it, but we can never know it fully or adequately. It is this background of ignorance, this unexhausted remainder always present to our feeling, that partly explains, as was suggested in the preceding lecture, the contrast we draw between the phenomenon, or the object as known, and the noumenon, or the object as it exists.

The noumenon is, in this sense, an ideal to which we are always approximating, but to which we never attain. It is this also which lends a certain dynamic impulse even to an abstraction apparently so barren as the Unknowable. The *Unknowable* would, indeed, be absolutely barren. But there mingles subtly with the conception the feeling of the *Unknown*, the not yet known, the vast unexplored possibilities of the universe; and thus the notion is half redeemed in spite of itself. It is to this fact, also, of the vast unknown, and not to the other supposed fact of unknowableness, that most of Hamilton's "cloud of witnesses" really refer. And Hamilton himself apparently does not observe the essential difference between the two positions; for he sums up at one point by saying that "the grand result of human wisdom is thus only a consciousness that what we know is as nothing to what we know not"—a confession which, it is to be hoped, we are all prepared to make with befitting humility.

What has been said of the inexhaustible nature of reality, and of the relation which our conceptions bear to things, ought to prepare even those who move on Hegelian lines for the admission, that the idea of an absolute Self-consciousness, in which thought achieves a view of the systematic unity of things, is to a certain extent an ideal. That is to say, it is something in which we cannot but believe, rather than something we actually see. It is not sufficient, in dealing with a point like this, merely to announce our adherence to one side or another. It is not enough to say, for example, that we are Hegelians or "Gnostics," simply because we accept the idea of an eternal self-realising consciousness as that in which alone philosophy can rest. It is essential to make explicit the precise sense in which we understand our own position, and the measure, or rather the manner, of certainty which we conceive to belong to it. Is our insight the insight that comes from complete review, from actual seeing? In other words, is it knowledge in the strict sense of that term? Or does it partake of the nature of divination and faith — divination through the application of principles which themselves lie within our grasp, and which (in spite of difficulties which we cannot personally resolve) we cannot but believe to supply the key to all the locks in Doubting Castle? This is the question, as between Gnosticism and the Philosophy of Faith, which is pressed home in the concluding chapter of a book which I hope it is not unbecoming in me to refer to here as being, to my mind, the ripest and most catholic expression of the national tendency in philosophy—I mean Professor Fraser's recent volume on Berkeley.[1]

The term Faith or Belief is one which is susceptible of many meanings and applications. I have already expressed my strong sense of the mischief which often attends it when introduced into philosophical discussion. We may go further, and say that wherever faith is pitted against reason, wherever an opposition is set up between the two—we might even say, wherever they are treated as separate or distinct organs—we are upon unsound ground, and mischief lurks not far distant. Faith is not used here, of course, in a distinctively theological sense; but in that reference also we found it impossible to treat theology as a back-door by which we might escape, in a trice, from all our philosophical difficulties. I hold it certain that a faith built upon what Hamilton calls the impotence—the imbecility—of reason, is built upon a foundation of sand; experience has shown us again and again that great is the fall thereof. Let us mistrust, therefore, let us deeply mistrust, any one who endeavours to set the apple of discord rolling between these two—any one who seeks to make capital

[1] In Blackwood's Philosophical Classics.

for the one out of the discomfiture of the other. Let us beware, as Plato says, of becoming misologues.

But we have now reached a point where faith and reason join hands on the utmost confines of speculation; and some further elucidation of terms is therefore desirable. The true antithesis is not so much between Faith and Reason as between Faith and Knowledge. Indeed the term Reason has sometimes been used—by Jacobi, for example—as equivalent to Faith, and as opposed, in that sense, to the Understanding, which then corresponds to our use of the term Knowledge. What the opposition really expresses is the difference between the attitude of the human mind towards the universe as a whole, and its attitude towards any definite part of it. In what sense can we say that we *know* the harmony of the whole, that we know the universe as a system? No one, I think, will say that we know or see it—that we have it actually before us—in the same sense in which we know some individual object, some particular tract of experience. We see, it will be said, that it must be so, that the system must complete itself in the manner indicated; we see that certain presuppositions are involved in or demanded by the facts under our hands, in such a way that our knowledge of these facts involves a knowledge of the synthesis which makes them intelligible. But this implies—may it not be answered—that the system does not complete itself *for me;* that I have not the harmonious plan outspread before me? Only by actually *being* God, could we have such a view of the universe as would entitle us to speak here of knowledge in the strict sense. If, then, I am ignorant (as I surely am in many cases) of the precise manner in which seemingly discordant elements are subordinated to the ultimate harmony, then the harmony itself may justifiably be spoken of as an object of faith—something which I am constrained to believe, even though I do not fully see it. If any one wishes to hear a full acknowledgment of this on the lips of one who certainly worked on the lines of Absolute Idealism, he has only to turn to passages like the following from Green's 'Prolegomena to Ethics,' or to many others in his Sermon on Faith: "There never can be that actual wholeness of the world for us, which there must be for the mind that renders the world one. But though the conditions under which the eternal consciousness reproduces itself in our knowledge are thus incompatible with finality in that knowledge, there is that element of identity between the first stage of intelligent experience and the eternal consciousness reproducing itself in it, which consists in the presentation of a many in one, in the apprehension of facts related in a single system, *in the conception of there being an order of things, whatever that order may turn out to be*. . . . It is only as governed by *the forecast of there being a related whole*, that the processes of sensuous experience can yield a growing, though for ever incomplete, knowledge of what in detail the whole is."[1] Here we have at once the fullest acknowledgment of the absence of perfect insight, and an insistence on the *necessity* of the faith. It is doubtless the prominence usually given by Absolute Idealists to the latter element, which has caused their position to be understood as if it implied a claim to personal omniscience. Many Hegelians talk and write as if they were in the happy position of having no difficulties. But this is not Green's tone. Passages like the foregoing, I cannot but think, go far to show that the difference between the Gnostics and the Faith-Philosophers is not so great as it at first sight appears, provided that both aim at sobriety of statement, and agree to define their terms. For

[1] Prolegomena to Ethics, p. 77.

we cannot afford to omit the "necessity" from our account of the faith; we must have grounds for our faith. There may be incongruities which we cannot weave into a consistent scheme; but we must have certain facts before us which *necessitate* us to adopt a certain hypothesis, even though we cannot see as yet how certain other refractory facts are to be reconciled with it. The facts for the explanation of which the hypothesis is required must be of so central and dominating a nature, that they justify our adhesion to it, even in spite of temporary anomalies. Such facts Green found in the necessary presence of a connective self-consciousness in order to constitute facts, and in the ethical "Thou shalt" which transforms the animal impulses into the organs of a reasonable life.

Scottish philosophy has hardly anything to say on this question of the possibility of systematic philosophy, or, to give it its old name, the possibility of Ontology. Not that it has anything to urge *in limine* against its possibility; for the Dualism, which is often put forward as the watchword and characteristic tenet of the school, has no direct bearing upon the question we are considering. The doctrine was not elaborated in view of the ultimate problem of the rational unity of the universe. It does not, therefore, denote the existence of an irrational surd in the problem —that is to say, the presence of some element impenetrable by reason, some element that refuses to be worked into the ultimate synthesis. In that sense, of course, Dualism would be simply another name for the paralysis of reason. But the Scottish doctrine was elaborated, we must remember, merely in reference to perception, and in the face of the ideal system and the theory of representationism. Only in that reference, therefore, can its statements be fairly interpreted. So taken, they are more pliable in the interests of rationalism than those of the theory to which they are opposed. For such dualism, as is asserted, is an opposition in which both the factors are known; whereas the representationists and relativists everywhere assert an opposition between mind and something which is essentially unapproachable by mind, and which might, therefore, be plausibly cited as an irreducible surd in the universe of being. This would be a really embarrassing dualism. The doctrine of Scottish philosophy, on the other hand, is better characterised by its other name of Natural Realism. What it asserts is a known reality on the one side and on the other. "I maintain," says Dr M'Cosh, "that just as, by self-consciousness, we know self as exercising such and such a quality—say, thinking or feeling—so, by sense-perception, we know a body as extended and exercising power or energy. This is the simplest doctrine, . . . and is the proper doctrine of natural realism as distinguished from an artificial system of relativity."[1] Unless this be all too grossly interpreted, it states a fact which only a weak-minded idealism would attempt to explain away. Hegel, at all events, rather delights in emphasising the fact of "otherness" or difference; he is fond of pointing out the relative independence of nature—the full swing, so to speak, in which it is indulged—as removing any suspicion of subjective idealism. He only adds that, ultimately or ontologically, the world is every way, as the poet says, "bound by gold chains about the feet of God": a position which the Scottish philosophers, in turn, would not have thought of questioning.

The Scottish philosophers, however, though their metaphysic of perception leaves them quite free, certainly do not occupy themselves to any large extent with the problems of Ontology—the

[1] Scottish Philosophy, p. 290.

problems, that is to say, of the ultimate nature and mutual relations of Self, the World, and God. Scottish philosophy, to borrow a phrase skilfully applied by Professor Masson,[1] has been almost entirely *cosmological* in character. It has stated, for example, the fact of dualism between subject and object as actually found in experience, without caring to attempt the further task of ontologically relating this dualism, if possible, to a principle of ultimate unity. For their personal ontology, if we may so speak, they simply fell back upon the language of religion, which relates God to the world as its Creator, and to man also as his Creator, and, in a special sense, his Father and his God. On that ground—the ground of religion—the Scottish philosophers are, therefore, as much Absolute Idealists as Hegel himself; for what is created enjoys only a dependent or derived existence. Religion, indeed, as Hegel says, is everywhere Idealism. It is the Sabbath of the spirit, the denial or correction of the crass realism of the workaday consciousness, the restoring of things to their true proportions by setting them in the light of the eternal and the Whole. But the religious treatment of such questions and the

[1] In his Recent British Philosophy.

philosophical treatment are not to be immediately identified. The organ of religion is faith; and whatever else faith may be, it is *not* completed insight, completed proof. It is the evidence of things not seen. A man may feel himself justified, therefore, in stating certain things when he is speaking within the sphere of religion, and yet shrink from incorporating them with his *ex cathedrâ* philosophical utterances. For philosophy, as philosophy, demands proof; it insists on having its statements thought out. It is not enough for the philosopher to believe that things *are* so; he must also see *how* they are so. He must be able to give some *rationale* of the process. Very probably, therefore, the neglect of the philosophers of our country to carry up their theories of the mind into an Ontology may be partly explained by an underlying conviction on their part that the problem of ontology carries us beyond the limits of knowledge in the strict sense of that word.

In any case, however, the omission proves clearly enough that they were not inspired by that unquenchable speculative ardour which has sent forth so many knights in quest of the philosophic Grail. And, look at it how we may, the absence of a native Ontology is a thing to be regretted. For the intellectual caution of our country might have helped us to step more warily, and to talk less pretentiously, than is sometimes the custom of the Germans from whom we have been compelled to borrow. Such a spirit of intellectual modesty and candour I recognise, for example, in the conclusion of an able book from which I have already quoted, —'Metaphysica Nova et Vetusta,'—published anonymously last year by an author who calls himself Scotus Novanticus.[1] "Change and pain, decay and death," he says, "these stern facts of Nature, have to be sublated into the idea of the universal law of God's working, and in that sublation, if not explained, yet so conceived from a universal standpoint, as to yield, to the eye of Faith at least, a possible harmony. To the eye of Reason, in the sphere of exact knowledge, evil will ever remain a mystery. We may state the fact of evil in terms which seem to explain it— the more abstract the better, of course, if we desire to seem to know; but, in whatever terms rendered, it is evil. . . . It certainly is not given to us, in this mortal state, 'to know even

[1] See note on p. 160.

as we are known,' and there will always be room for the *faith* that 'all things work together for good to them that love God.'"

Such a close is more human than professed demonstrations, which sometimes strike us, after all, as only what this writer calls "seeming to know." In general, I think a Scottish metaphysic would have agreed with Lotze that, while holding with indestructible confidence to the belief that the universe has a *meaning*, on which its *existence* ultimately depends, "we do not know this meaning in its fulness, and therefore we cannot deduce from it, what we can only attempt, in one universal conviction, to retrace to it."[1] In other words, it would have reversed the deductive method which we find in Fichte and Hegel. The ultimate unity of things is what we stretch forward to, what we divine, but what we never fully attain. It is our *terminus ad quem;* it is never so fully within our grasp that we can make it in turn our *terminus a quo*, and, placing ourselves, as it were, at the crisis of creation, proceed to deduce step by step the characteristics of actual existence in nature and in man. Wherever Hegel or any one else appears to adopt such a method

[1] Metaphysics, p. 536 (English translation).

of procedure, we find, I think, that the show of explanation is wholly illusory. Hegel carries us almost always with him *except* at such points—except where he seems to imply a perfect knowledge of a perfect world. The only human attitude, on the contrary, must be, starting from experience, amid much apparent imperfection and evil, to work towards a solution or satisfying explanation. Such a schema of explanation is to be found, as our examination of these two lines of philosophical thought has taught us, in the Self-consciousness which exhibits itself as a necessary principle of unity in all knowledge, and as a necessary form of law in all action.

But when we have said this, we must admit that many things have been left vague. What are we to say of the nature of this Self-consciousness which we call eternal? Has it an existence for itself, or is it realised only in the individuals whose thought it co-ordinates? And what of my own individual existence, and its relation to this eternal or universal consciousness? Hegelianism treats man simply as he is a universal or perceptive consciousness, gazing at the spectacle of things. In that process, the individual is, as it were, merged in the universal; we occupy, for the time, a universal standpoint, and it is quite indifferent whether it is my Ego or another that surveys the world. But a philosophy which goes no further than this in its treatment of the individual, leaves untouched what we may call the individual in the individual — those subjective memories, thoughts, and plans which make each of us a separate soul. The vague answers of Hegelianism on such points, and on the connected question of immortality, are proofs that, in many respects, it belies its name of Gnosticism; there is a great deal which it does not know. If it tries, as it does in some of its representatives, to ignore these questions as unimportant, it is to be strenuously resisted; for there it makes common cause with dogmatic Materialism and Positivism, and is included, therefore, in Lotze's censure of the spirit of negative resignation current in certain circles—that heroism, spurious as it is frail, which prides itself on being able to renounce what never *ought* to be renounced.[1] Here, without doubt, in the questions of individual destiny, will always be found the great sphere of philosophic faith—a faith which can no longer depend on any consideration of the soul as an indivisible substance, but must rest ultimately on our doctrine of God. But the record of philosophy is

[1] Preface to the Mikrokosmos.

not closed; and an advance may yet be made towards greater philosophical precision, by any one who will endeavour to repair the omissions of Hegelian universalism in respect of the individual, and the nature of the existence that belongs to it.

THE END.

PRINTED BY WILLIAM BLACKWOOD AND SONS.

# PHILOSOPHICAL WORKS.

LECTURES ON METAPHYSICS. By Sir WILLIAM HAMILTON, Bart., Professor of Logic and Metaphysics in the University of Edinburgh. Seventh Edition. Edited by the Very Rev. H. L. MANSELL, LL.D., Dean of St Paul's, and JOHN VEITCH, M.A., Professor of Logic and Rhetoric, Glasgow. 2 vols. 8vo. 24s.

LECTURES ON LOGIC. By Sir WILLIAM HAMILTON, Bart. Third Edition. Edited by the Same. 2 vols. 8vo. 24s.

DISCUSSIONS ON PHILOSOPHY AND LITERATURE, EDUCATION AND UNIVERSITY REFORM. By Sir WILLIAM HAMILTON, BART. Third Edition. 8vo. 21s.

METHOD, MEDITATIONS, AND PRINCIPLES OF PHILOSOPHY OF DESCARTES. Translated from the original French and Latin. With a New Introductory Essay, Historical and Critical, on the Cartesian Philosophy. By JOHN VEITCH, LL.D., Professor of Logic and Rhetoric in the University of Glasgow. Eighth Edition. 12mo. 6s. 6d.

PHILOSOPHICAL WORKS OF THE LATE JAMES FREDERICK FERRIER, B.A. Oxon., LL.D., Professor of Moral Philosophy and Political Economy in the University of St Andrews. New Edition. 3 vols. crown 8vo. 34s. 6d.

The following are sold Separately :—

INSTITUTES OF METAPHYSIC. Third Edition. 10s. 6d.

LECTURES ON THE EARLY GREEK PHILOSOPHY. New Edition. 10s. 6d.

PHILOSOPHICAL REMAINS, INCLUDING THE LECTURES ON EARLY GREEK PHILOSOPHY. Edited by Sir ALEX. GRANT, Bart., D.C.L., and Professor LUSHINGTON. 2 vols. 24s.

*IN COURSE OF PUBLICATION.*

PHILOSOPHICAL CLASSICS FOR ENGLISH READERS. EDITED BY PROFESSOR KNIGHT, LL.D., St Andrews. In crown 8vo Volumes, with Portraits, price 3s. 6d.

*Now ready—*

1. DESCARTES. By Professor MAHAFFY, Dublin.
2. BUTLER. By Rev. W. LUCAS COLLINS, M.A.
3. BERKELEY. By Professor CAMPBELL FRASER, Edinburgh.
4. FICHTE. By Professor ADAMSON, Owens College, Manchester.
5. KANT. By Professor WALLACE, Oxford.
6. HAMILTON. By Professor VEITCH, Glasgow.
7. HEGEL. By Professor EDWARD CAIRD, Glasgow.
8. LEIBNIZ. By JOHN THEODORE MERZ.
9. VICO. By Professor FLINT, Edinburgh.
10. HOBBES. By Professor CROOM ROBERTSON, London.

*In preparation—*

HUME. By the Editor. | SPINOZA. By the Very Rev. Principal
BACON. By Prof. NICHOL, Glasgow. | CAIRD, Glasgow.

WILLIAM BLACKWOOD & SONS, EDINBURGH AND LONDON.

# NEW PUBLICATIONS.

ON THE ETHICS OF NATURALISM. Being the SHAW FELLOWSHIP LECTURES, 1884. By W. R. SORLEY, M.A., Fellow of Trinity College, Cambridge; and Examiner in Philosophy in the University of Edinburgh. Crown 8vo, 6s.

MODERN THEORIES IN PHILOSOPHY AND RELIGION. By JOHN TULLOCH, D.D., LL.D., Principal of St Mary's College in the University of St Andrews; and one of her Majesty's Chaplains in Ordinary in Scotland. 8vo, 15s.

CAN THE OLD FAITH LIVE WITH THE NEW? OR, THE PROBLEM OF EVOLUTION AND REVELATION. By the REV. GEORGE MATHESON, D.D., Innellan. Crown 8vo, 7s. 6d.

### A NEW EDITION, REVISED.

CHARACTERISTICS OF ENGLISH POETS FROM CHAUCER TO SHIRLEY. By WILLIAM MINTO, M.A., Professor of Logic and English Literature in the University of Aberdeen. Second Edition. Crown 8vo, 7s. 6d.

A MANUAL OF ENGLISH PROSE LITERATURE, BIOGRAPHICAL AND CRITICAL. DESIGNED MAINLY TO SHOW CHARACTERISTICS OF STYLE. By the SAME. New and Cheaper Edition, Revised. Crown 8vo, 7s. 6d.

GREEK TESTAMENT LESSONS FOR COLLEGES, SCHOOLS, AND PRIVATE STUDENTS, consisting chiefly of The Sermon on the Mount, and the Parables of our Lord. With Notes and Essays. By the REV. J. HUNTER SMITH, M.A., King Edward's School, Birmingham; formerly Scholar of Merton College, Oxford. With 4 Maps. Crown 8vo, 6s.

### IN ONE VOLUME, THE LIBRARY EDITION.

A DICTIONARY OF THE ENGLISH LANGUAGE, PRONOUNCING, ETYMOLOGICAL, AND EXPLANATORY, Embracing Scientific and other Terms, Numerous Familiar Terms, and a Copious Selection of Old English Words. By the REV. JAMES STORMONTH. The PRONUNCIATION carefully revised by the Rev. P. H. PHELP, M.A., Cantab. Royal 8vo. Handsomely bound in half-morocco, 31s. 6d.

"May serve in a great measure the purposes of an English cyclopedia."—*Times*.

"One of the best and most serviceable works of reference of its class."—*Scotsman*.

"The work exhibits all the freshness and best results of modern lexicographic scholarship."—*New York Tribune*.

WILLIAM BLACKWOOD & SONS, EDINBURGH AND LONDON.

# CATALOGUE

OF

# MESSRS BLACKWOOD & SONS' PUBLICATIONS.

# PHILOSOPHICAL CLASSICS FOR ENGLISH READERS.
### Edited by WILLIAM KNIGHT, LL.D.,
Professor of Moral Philosophy in the University of St Andrews.

In crown 8vo Volumes, with Portraits, price 3s. 6d.

*Now ready—*

1. **Descartes.** By Professor MAHAFFY, Dublin.
2. **Butler.** By Rev. W. LUCAS COLLINS, M.A.
3. **Berkeley.** By Professor FRASER, Edinburgh.
4. **Fichte.** By Professor ADAMSON, Owens College, Manchester.
5. **Kant.** By Professor WALLACE, Oxford.
6. **Hamilton.** By Professor VEITCH, Glasgow.
7. **Hegel.** By Professor EDWARD CAIRD, Glasgow.
8. **Leibniz.** By J. THEODORE MERZ.
9. **Vico.** By Professor FLINT, Edinburgh.
10. **Hobbes.** By Professor CROOM ROBERTSON, London.

*The Volumes in preparation are—*

HUME. By the Editor.  
BACON. By Professor Nichol, Glasgow.  
SPINOZA. By the Very Rev. Principal Caird, Glasgow.

---

IN COURSE OF PUBLICATION.

# FOREIGN CLASSICS FOR ENGLISH READERS.
### Edited by Mrs OLIPHANT.

In Crown 8vo, 2s. 6d.

*The Volumes published are—*

DANTE. By the Editor.  
VOLTAIRE. By Major-General Sir E. B. Hamley, K.C.M.G.  
PASCAL. By Principal Tulloch.  
PETRARCH. By Henry Reeve, C.B.  
GOETHE. By A. Hayward, Q.C.  
MOLIÈRE. By the Editor and F. Tarver, M.A.  
MONTAIGNE. By Rev. W. L. Collins, M.A.  
RABELAIS. By Walter Besant, M.A.  
CALDERON. By E. J. Hasell.  
SAINT SIMON. By Clifton W. Collins, M.A.  
CERVANTES. By the Editor.  
CORNEILLE AND RACINE. By Henry M. Trollope.  
MADAME DE SÉVIGNÉ. By Miss Thackeray.  
LA FONTAINE, AND OTHER FRENCH FABULISTS. By Rev. W. Lucas Collins, M.A.  
SCHILLER. By James Sime, M.A., Author of 'Lessing: his Life and Writings.'  
TASSO. By E. J. Hasell.  
ROUSSEAU. By Henry Grey Graham.

*In preparation—*LEOPARDI, by the Editor.

---

Now Complete.

# ANCIENT CLASSICS FOR ENGLISH READERS.
### Edited by the Rev. W. LUCAS COLLINS, M.A.

Complete in 28 Vols. crown 8vo, cloth, price 2s. 6d. each. And may also be had in 14 Volumes, strongly and neatly bound, with calf or vellum back, £3, 10s.

*Saturday Review.*—"It is difficult to estimate too highly the value of such a series as this in giving 'English readers' an insight, exact as far as it goes, into those olden times which are so remote and yet to many of us so close."

# CATALOGUE

OF

# MESSRS BLACKWOOD & SONS'
## PUBLICATIONS.

---

ALISON. History of Europe. By Sir ARCHIBALD ALISON, Bart., D.C.L.
1. From the Commencement of the French Revolution to the Battle of Waterloo.
    LIBRARY EDITION, 14 vols., with Portraits. Demy 8vo, £10, 10s.
    ANOTHER EDITION, in 20 vols. crown 8vo, £6.
    PEOPLE'S EDITION, 13 vols. crown 8vo, £2, 11s.
2. Continuation to the Accession of Louis Napoleon.
    LIBRARY EDITION, 8 vols. 8vo, £6, 7s. 6d.
    PEOPLE'S EDITION, 8 vols. crown 8vo, 34s.
3. Epitome of Alison's History of Europe. Twenty-ninth Thousand, 7s. 6d.
4. Atlas to Alison's History of Europe. By A. Keith Johnston.
    LIBRARY EDITION, demy 4to, £3, 3s.
    PEOPLE'S EDITION, 31s. 6d.

------ Life of John Duke of Marlborough. With some Account of his Contemporaries, and of the War of the Succession. Third Edition, 2 vols. 8vo. Portraits and Maps, 30s.

------ Essays: Historical, Political, and Miscellaneous. 3 vols. demy 8vo, 45s.

------ Lives of Lord Castlereagh and Sir Charles Stewart, Second and Third Marquesses of Londonderry. From the Original Paper of the Family. 3 vols. 8vo, £2, 2s.

ADAMS. Great Campaigns. A Succinct Account of the Principal Military Operations which have taken place in Europe from 1796 to 1870. By Major C. ADAMS, Professor of Military History at the Staff College. Edited by Captain C. COOPER KING, R.M. Artillery, Instructor of Tactics, Royal Military College. 8vo, with Maps. 16s.

AIRD. Poetical Works of Thomas Aird. Fifth Edition, with Memoir of the Author by the Rev. JARDINE WALLACE, and Portrait. Crown 8vo, 7s. 6d.

ALLARDYCE. The City of Sunshine. By ALEXANDER ALLARDYCE. Three vols. post 8vo, £1, 5s. 6d.

------ Memoir of the Honourable George Keith Elphinstone, K.B., Viscount Keith of Stonehaven Marischal, Admiral of the Red. One vol. 8vo, with Portrait, Illustrations, and Maps. 21s.

**ANCIENT CLASSICS FOR ENGLISH READERS.** Edited by Rev. W. LUCAS COLLINS, M.A. Complete in 28 vols., cloth, 2s. 6d. each; or in 14 vols., tastefully bound, with calf or vellum back, £3, 10s.

*Contents of the Series.*

HOMER: THE ILIAD. By the Editor.
HOMER: THE ODYSSEY. By the Editor.
HERODOTUS. By George C. Swayne, M.A.
XENOPHON. By Sir Alexander Grant, Bart., LL.D.
EURIPIDES. By W. B. Donne.
ARISTOPHANES. By the Editor.
PLATO. By Clifton W. Collins, M.A.
LUCIAN. By the Editor.
ÆSCHYLUS. By the Right Rev. the Bishop of Colombo.
SOPHOCLES. By Clifton W. Collins, M.A.
HESIOD AND THEOGNIS. By the Rev. J. Davies, M.A.
GREEK ANTHOLOGY. By Lord Neaves.
VIRGIL. By the Editor.
HORACE. By Sir Theodore Martin, K.C.B.
JUVENAL. By Edward Walford, M.A.
PLAUTUS AND TERENCE. By the Editor.
THE COMMENTARIES OF CÆSAR. By Anthony Trollope.
TACITUS. By W. B. Donne.
CICERO. By the Editor.
PLINY'S LETTERS. By the Rev. Alfred Church, M.A., and the Rev. W. J. Brodribb, M.A.
LIVY. By the Editor.
OVID. By the Rev. A. Church, M.A.
CATULLUS, TIBULLUS, AND PROPERTIUS. By the Rev. Jas. Davies, M.A.
DEMOSTHENES. By the Rev. W. J. Brodribb, M.A.
ARISTOTLE. By Sir Alexander Grant, Bart., LL.D.
THUCYDIDES. By the Editor.
LUCRETIUS. By W. H. Mallock, M.A.
PINDAR. By the Rev. F. D. Morice, M.A.

**AYLWARD.** The Transvaal of To-day: War, Witchcraft, Sports, and Spoils in South Africa. By ALFRED AYLWARD, Commandant, Transvaal Republic; Captain (late) Lydenberg Volunteer Corps. Second Edition. Crown 8vo, with a Map, 6s.

**AYTOUN.** Lays of the Scottish Cavaliers, and other Poems. By W. EDMONDSTOUNE AYTOUN, D.C.L., Professor of Rhetoric and Belles-Lettres in the University of Edinburgh. Twenty-ninth Edition. Fcap. 8vo, 7s. 6d.

—— An Illustrated Edition of the Lays of the Scottish Cavaliers. From designs by Sir NOEL PATON. Small 4to, 21s., in gilt cloth.

—— Bothwell: a Poem. Third Edition. Fcap., 7s. 6d.

—— Firmilian; or, The Student of Badajoz. A Spasmodic Tragedy. Fcap., 5s.

—— Poems and Ballads of Goethe. Translated by Professor AYTOUN and Sir THEODORE MARTIN, K.C.B. Third Edition. Fcap., 6s.

—— Bon Gaultier's Book of Ballads. By the SAME. Fourteenth and Cheaper Edition. With Illustrations by Doyle, Leech, and Crowquill. Fcap. 8vo, 5s.

—— The Ballads of Scotland. Edited by Professor AYTOUN. Fourth Edition. 2 vols. fcap. 8vo, 12s.

—— Memoir of William E. Aytoun, D.C.L. By Sir THEODORE MARTIN, K.C.B. With Portrait. Post 8vo, 12s.

**BACH.** On Musical Education and Vocal Culture. By ALBERT B. BACH. Fourth Edition. 8vo, 7s. 6d.

—— The Principles and Practice of Singing. With numerous Vocal Exercises. In one volume. Crown 8vo. [*In the press.*

**BALLADS AND POEMS.** By MEMBERS OF THE GLASGOW BALLAD CLUB. Crown 8vo, 7s. 6d.

**BATTLE OF DORKING.** Reminiscences of a Volunteer. From 'Blackwood's Magazine.' Second Hundredth Thousand. 6d.

**BEDFORD.** The Regulations of the Old Hospital of the Knights of St John at Valetta. From a Copy Printed at Rome, and preserved in the Archives of Malta; with a Translation, Introduction, and Notes Explanatory of the Hospital Work of the Order. By the Rev. W. K. R. BEDFORD, one of the Chaplains of the Order of St John in England. Royal 8vo, with Frontispiece, Plans, &c., 7s. 6d.

BELLAIRS. The Transvaal War, 1880-81. Edited by Lady BEL-
LAIRS. With a Frontispiece and Map. 8vo, 15s.

BESANT. The Revolt of Man. By WALTER BESANT, M.A.
Seventh Edition. Crown 8vo, 3s. 6d.

——— Readings in Rabelais. Crown 8vo, 7s. 6d.

BEVERIDGE. Culross and Tulliallan; or Perthshire on Forth. Its
History and Antiquities. With Elucidations of Scottish Life and Character
from the Burgh and Kirk-Session Records of that District. By DAVID
BEVERIDGE. 2 vols. 8vo, with Illustrations, 42s.

BLACKIE. Lays and Legends of Ancient Greece. By JOHN
STUART BLACKIE, Emeritus Professor of Greek in the University of Edinburgh. Second Edition. Fcap. 8vo. 5s.

——— The Wisdom of Goethe. Fcap. 8vo. Cloth, extra gilt, 6s.

BLACKWOOD'S MAGAZINE, from Commencement in 1817 to
December 1883. Nos. 1 to 818, forming 134 Volumes.

——— Index to Blackwood's Magazine. Vols. 1 to 50. 8vo, 15s.

——— Tales from Blackwood. Forming Twelve Volumes of
Interesting and Amusing Railway Reading. Price One Shilling each in Paper
Cover. Sold separately at all Railway Bookstalls.
They may also be had bound in cloth, 18s., and in half calf, richly gilt, 30s.
or 12 volumes in 6, Roxburghe, 21s., and half red morocco, 28s.

——— Tales from Blackwood. New Series. Complete in Twenty-
four Shilling Parts. Handsomely bound in 12 vols., cloth, 30s. In leather
back, Roxburghe style, 37s. 6d. In half calf, gilt, 52s. 6d. In half morocco, 55s.

——— Standard Novels. Uniform in size and legibly Printed.
Each Novel complete in one volume.

Florin Series, Illustrated Boards.

TOM CRINGLE'S LOG. By Michael Scott.
THE CRUISE OF THE MIDGE. By the Same.
CYRIL THORNTON. By Captain Hamilton.
ANNALS OF THE PARISH. By John Galt.
THE PROVOST, &c. By John Galt.
SIR ANDREW WYLIE. By John Galt.
THE ENTAIL. By John Galt.
MISS MOLLY. By Beatrice May Butt.
REGINALD DALTON. By J. G. Lockhart.

PEN OWEN. By Dean Hook.
ADAM BLAIR. By J. G. Lockhart.
LADY LEE'S WIDOWHOOD. By General
Sir E. B. Hamley.
SALEM CHAPEL. By Mrs Oliphant.
THE PERPETUAL CURATE. By Mrs Oli-
phant.
MISS MARJORIBANKS. By Mrs Oliphant.
JOHN: A Love Story. By Mrs Oliphant.

Or in Cloth Boards, 2s. 6d.

Shilling Series, Illustrated Cover.

THE RECTOR, and THE DOCTOR'S FAMILY.
By Mrs Oliphant.
THE LIFE OF MANSIE WAUCH. By D. M.
Moir.
PENINSULAR SCENES AND SKETCHES. By
F. Hardman.

SIR FRIZZLE PUMPKIN, NIGHTS AT MESS,
&c.
THE SUBALTERN.
LIFE IN THE FAR WEST. By G. F. Ruxton.
VALERIUS: A Roman Story. By J. G.
Lockhart.

Or in Cloth Boards, 1s. 6d.

BLACKMORE. The Maid of Sker. By R. D. BLACKMORE, Author
of 'Lorna Doone,' &c. Tenth Edition. Crown 8vo, 7s. 6d.

BOSCOBEL TRACTS. Relating to the Escape of Charles the
Second after the Battle of Worcester, and his subsequent Adventures. Edited
by J. HUGHES, Esq., A.M. A New Edition, with additional Notes and Illustrations, including Communications from the Rev. R. H. BARHAM, Author of
the 'Ingoldsby Legends.' 8vo, with Engravings, 16s.

BRACKENBURY. A Narrative of the Ashanti War. Prepared
from the official documents, by permission of General Lord Wolseley, G.C.B.,
G.C.M.G. By Major-General H. BRACKENBURY, C.B. With Maps from the
latest Surveys made by the Staff of the Expedition. 2 vols. 8vo, 25s.

BRACKENBURY. The River Column: A Narrative of the Advance of the River Column of the Nile Expeditionary Force, and its Return down the Rapids. By Major-General HENRY BRACKENBURY, C.B., Late Commanding the River Column With Maps by Major the Hon. F. L. L. COLBORNE, Royal Irish Rifles. Crown 8vo, 7s. 6d.

BROADLEY. Tunis, Past and Present. With a Narrative of the French Conquest of the Regency. By A. M. BROADLEY. With numerous Illustrations and Maps. 2 vols. post 8vo. 25s.

BROOKE, Life of Sir James, Rajah of Sarāwak. From his Personal Papers and Correspondence. By SPENSER ST JOHN, H.M.'s Minister-Resident and Consul-General Peruvian Republic; formerly Secretary to the Rajah. With Portrait and a Map. Post 8vo, 12s. 6d.

BROUGHAM. Memoirs of the Life and Times of Henry Lord Brougham. Written by HIMSELF. 3 vols. 8vo, £2, 8s. The Volumes are sold separately, price 16s. each.

BROWN. The Forester: A Practical Treatise on the Planting, Rearing, and General Management of Forest-trees. By JAMES BROWN, LL.D., Inspector of and Reporter on Woods and Forests, Benmore House, Port Elgin, Ontario. Fifth Edition, revised and enlarged. Royal 8vo, with Engravings. 36s.

BROWN. The Ethics of George Eliot's Works. By JOHN CROMBIE BROWN. Fourth Edition. Crown 8vo, 2s. 6d.

BROWN. A Manual of Botany, Anatomical and Physiological. For the Use of Students. By ROBERT BROWN, M.A., Ph.D. Crown 8vo, with numerous Illustrations, 12s. 6d.

BUCHAN. Introductory Text-Book of Meteorology. By ALEXANDER BUCHAN, M.A., F.R.S.E., Secretary of the Scottish Meteorological Society, &c. Crown 8vo, with 8 Coloured Charts and other Engravings, pp. 218. 4s. 6d.

BURBIDGE. Domestic Floriculture, Window Gardening, and Floral Decorations. Being practical directions for the Propagation, Culture, and Arrangement of Plants and Flowers as Domestic Ornaments. By F. W. BURBIDGE. Second Edition. Crown 8vo, with numerous Illustrations, 7s. 6d.

——— Cultivated Plants: Their Propagation and Improvement. Including Natural and Artificial Hybridisation, Raising from Seed, Cuttings, and Layers, Grafting and Budding, as applied to the Families and Genera in Cultivation. Crown 8vo, with numerous Illustrations, 12s. 6d.

BURTON. The History of Scotland: From Agricola's Invasion to the Extinction of the last Jacobite Insurrection. By JOHN HILL BURTON, D.C.L., Historiographer-Royal for Scotland. New and Enlarged Edition, 8 vols., and Index. Crown 8vo, £3, 3s.

——— History of the British Empire during the Reign of Queen Anne. In 3 vols. 8vo. 36s.

——— The Scot Abroad. New Edition. Crown 8vo, 10s. 6d.

——— The Book-Hunter. New Edition. Crown 8vo, 7s. 6d.

BUTE. The Roman Breviary: Reformed by Order of the Holy Œcumenical Council of Trent; Published by Order of Pope St Pius V.; and Revised by Clement VIII. and Urban VIII.; together with the Offices since granted. Translated out of Latin into English by JOHN, Marquess of Bute, K.T. In 2 vols. crown 8vo, cloth boards, edges uncut. £2, 2s.

——— The Altus of St Columba. With a Prose Paraphrase and Notes. In paper cover, 2s. 6d.

BUTT. Miss Molly. By BEATRICE MAY BUTT. Cheap Edition, 2s.

——— Geraldine Hawthorne: A Sketch. By the Author of 'Miss Molly.' Crown 8vo, 7s. 6d.

BUTT. Alison. By the Author of 'Miss Molly.' 3 vols. crown 8vo, 25s. 6d.

CAIRD. Sermons. By JOHN CAIRD, D.D., Principal of the University of Glasgow. Sixteenth Thousand. Fcap. 8vo, 5s.

—— Religion in Common Life. A Sermon preached in Crathie Church, October 14, 1855, before Her Majesty the Queen and Prince Albert. Published by Her Majesty's Command. Cheap Edition, 3d.

CAMERON. Gaelic Names of Plants (Scottish and Irish). Collected and Arranged in Scientific Order, with Notes on their Etymology, their Uses, Plant Superstitions, &c., among the Celts, with copious Gaelic, English, and Scientific Indices. By JOHN CAMERON, Sunderland. 8vo, 7s. 6d.

CAMPBELL. Sermons Preached before the Queen at Balmoral. By the Rev. A. A. CAMPBELL, Minister of Crathie. Published by Command of Her Majesty. Crown 8vo, 4s. 6d.

CAMPBELL. Records of Argyll. Legends, Traditions, and Recollections of Argyllshire Highlanders, collected chiefly from the Gaelic. With Notes on the Antiquity of the Dress, Clan Colours or Tartans of the Highlanders. By LORD ARCHIBALD CAMPBELL. Illustrated with Nineteen full-page Etchings. 4to, printed on hand-made paper, £3, 3s.

CAPPON. Victor Hugo. A Memoir and a Study. By JAMES CAPPON, M.A. Post 8vo, 10s 6d.

CARRICK. Koumiss; or, Fermented Mare's Milk: and its Uses in the Treatment and Cure of Pulmonary Consumption, and other Wasting Diseases. With an Appendix on the best Methods of Fermenting Cow's Milk. By GEORGE L. CARRICK, M.D., L.R.C.S.E. and L.R.C.P.E., Physician to the British Embassy, St Petersburg, &c. Crown 8vo, 10s. 6d.

CAUVIN. A Treasury of the English and German Languages. Compiled from the best Authors and Lexicographers in both Languages. Adapted to the Use of Schools, Students, Travellers, and Men of Business; and forming a Companion to all German-English Dictionaries. By JOSEPH CAUVIN, LL.D. & Ph.D., of the University of Göttingen, &c. Crown 8vo, 7s. 6d.

CAVE-BROWN. Lambeth Palace and its Associations. By J. CAVE-BROWN, M.A., Vicar of Detling, Kent, and for many years Curate of Lambeth Parish Church. With an Introduction by the Archbishop of Canterbury. Second Edition, containing an additional Chapter on Medieval Life in the Old Palaces. 8vo, with Illustrations, 21s.

CHARTERIS. Canonicity; or, Early Testimonies to the Existence and Use of the Books of the New Testament. Based on Kirchhoffer's 'Quellensammlung.' Edited by A. H. CHARTERIS, D.D., Professor of Biblical Criticism in the University of Edinburgh. 8vo, 18s.

CHEVELEY NOVELS, THE.
    I. A MODERN MINISTER. 2 vols. With Twenty-six Illustrations. 17s.
    II. SAUL WEIR. 2 vols. With Twelve Illustrations by F. Barnard. 16s.

CHIROL. 'Twixt Greek and Turk. By M. VALENTINE CHIROL. Post 8vo. With Frontispiece and Map, 10s. 6d.

CHRISTISON. Life of Sir Robert Christison, Bart., M.D., D.C.L. Oxon., Professor of Medical Jurisprudence in the University of Edinburgh. Edited by his Sons. In two vols. 8vo. Vol. I—Autobiography. Vol. II.—Memoirs. [In the press.

CHURCH SERVICE SOCIETY. A Book on Common Order: Being Forms of Worship issued by the Church Service Society. Fourth Edition, 6s.

COCHRAN. A Handy Text-Book of Military Law. Compiled chiefly to assist Officers preparing for Examination; also for all Officers of the Regular and Auxiliary Forces. Specially arranged according to the Syllabus of Subjects of Examination for Promotion, Queen's Regulations, 1883. Comprising also a Synopsis of part of the Army Act. By MAJOR F. COCHRAN, Hampshire Regiment, Garrison Instructor, North British District. Crown 8vo, 7s. 6d.

LIST OF BOOKS PUBLISHED BY

COLQUHOUN. The Moor and the Loch. Containing Minute Instructions in all Highland Sports, with Wanderings over Crag and Corrie, Flood and Fell. By JOHN COLQUHOUN. Sixth Edition, greatly enlarged. With Illustrations. 2 vols. post 8vo, 26s.

COTTERILL. The Genesis of the Church. By the Right. Rev. HENRY COTTERILL, D.D., Bishop of Edinburgh. Demy 8vo, 16s.

COTTERILL. Suggested Reforms in Public Schools. By C. C. COTTERILL, M.A., Assistant Master at Fettes College, Edin. Crown 8vo, 3s. 6d.

CRANSTOUN. The Elegies of Albius Tibullus. Translated into English Verse, with Life of the Poet, and Illustrative Notes. By JAMES CRANSTOUN, LL.D., Author of a Translation of 'Catullus.' Crown 8vo, 6s. 6d.

—— The Elegies of Sextus Propertius. Translated into English Verse, with Life of the Poet, and Illustrative Notes. Crown 8vo, 7s. 6d.

CRAWFORD. The Doctrine of Holy Scripture respecting the Atonement. By the late THOMAS J. CRAWFORD, D.D., Professor of Divinity in the University of Edinburgh. Third Edition. 8vo, 12s.

—— The Fatherhood of God, Considered in its General and Special Aspects, and particularly in relation to the Atonement, with a Review of Recent Speculations on the Subject. Third Edition, Revised and Enlarged. 8vo, 9s.

—— The Preaching of the Cross, and other Sermons. 8vo, 7s. 6d.

—— The Mysteries of Christianity. Crown 8vo, 7s. 6d.

DAVIES. A Book of Thoughts for every Day in the Year. Selected from the Writings of the Rev. J. LLEWELLYN DAVIES, M.A. By Two CLERGYMEN. Fcap. 8vo, 3s. 6d.

DAVIES. Norfolk Broads and Rivers; or, The Waterways, Lagoons, and Decoys of East Anglia. By G. CHRISTOPHER DAVIES, Author of 'The Swan and her Crew.' Illustrated with Seven full-page Plates. New and Cheaper Edition. Crown 8vo, 6s.

DE AINSLIE. Life as I have Found It. By General DE AINSLIE. Post 8vo, 12s. 6d.

DESCARTES. The Method, Meditations, and Principles of Philosophy of Descartes. Translated from the Original French and Latin. With a New Introductory Essay, Historical and Critical, on the Cartesian Philosophy. By JOHN VEITCH, LL.D., Professor of Logic and Rhetoric in the University of Glasgow. A New Edition, being the Eighth. Price 6s. 6d.

DIDON. The Germans. By the Rev. Father DIDON, of the Order of Preaching Friars. Translated into English by RAPHAEL LEDOS DE BEAUFORT. Crown 8vo, 7s. 6d.

DOGS, OUR DOMESTICATED: Their Treatment in reference to Food, Diseases, Habits, Punishment, Accomplishments. By 'MAGENTA.' Crown 8vo, 2s. 6d.

DU CANE. The Odyssey of Homer, Books I.-XII. Translated into English Verse. By Sir CHARLES DU CANE, K.C.M.G. 8vo, 10s. 6d.

DUDGEON. History of the Edinburgh or Queen's Regiment Light Infantry Militia, now 3rd Battalion The Royal Scots; with an Account of the Origin and Progress of the Militia, and a Brief Sketch of the old Royal Scots. By Major R. C. DUDGEON, Adjutant 3rd Battalion The Royal Scots. Post 8vo, with Illustrations, 10s. 6d.

DUNSMORE. Manual of the Law of Scotland, as to the Relations between Agricultural Tenants and their Landlords, Servants, Merchants, and Bowers. By W. DUNSMORE, Advocate. In one vol. 8vo. [In the press.

DUPRE. Thoughts on Art, and Autobiographical Memoirs of Giovanni Dupré. Translated from the Italian by E. M. PERUZZI, with the permission of the Author. Crown 8vo, 10s. 6d.

ELIOT. George Eliot's Life, Related in her Letters and Journals. Arranged and Edited by her husband, J. W. Cross. With Portrait and other Illustrations. Third Edition. 3 vols. post 8vo, 42s.
——— Essays. By GEORGE ELIOT. Revised by the Author for publication. Post 8vo, 10s. 6d.
——— Novels by GEORGE ELIOT. Cheap Edition. Adam Bede. Illustrated. 3s. 6d., cloth.—The Mill on the Floss. Illustrated. 3s. 6d., cloth.—Scenes of Clerical Life. Illustrated. 3s., cloth.—Silas Marner: The Weaver of Raveloe. Illustrated. 2s. 6d., cloth.—Felix Holt, the Radical. Illustrated. 3s. 6d., cloth.—Romola. With Vignette. 3s. 6d., cloth.
——— Middlemarch. Crown 8vo, 7s. 6d.
——— Daniel Deronda. Crown 8vo, 7s. 6d.
——— Works of George Eliot (Cabinet Edition). Handsomely printed in a new type, 20 volumes, crown 8vo, price £5. The Volumes are also sold separately, price 5s. each, viz.:—
Romola. 2 vols.—Silas Marner, The Lifted Veil, Brother Jacob. 1 vol.—Adam Bede. 2 vols.—Scenes of Clerical Life. 2 vols.—The Mill on the Floss. 2 vols.—Felix Holt. 2 vols.—Middlemarch. 3 vols.—Daniel Deronda. 3 vols.—The Spanish Gypsy. 1 vol.—Jubal, and other Poems, Old and New. 1 vol.—Theophrastus Such. 1 vol.
——— Life of George Eliot. Cabinet Edition. With Portrait and other Illustrations. 3 vols. crown 8vo, 15s.
——— The Spanish Gypsy. Crown 8vo, 5s.
——— The Legend of Jubal, and other Poems, Old and New. New Edition. Fcap. 8vo, 5s., cloth.
——— Impressions of Theophrastus Such. New Edition. Crown 8vo, 5s.
——— Wise, Witty, and Tender Sayings, in Prose and Verse. Selected from the Works of GEORGE ELIOT. Sixth Edition. Fcap. 8vo, 6s.
——— The George Eliot Birthday Book. Printed on fine paper, with red border, and handsomely bound in cloth, gilt. Fcap. 8vo, cloth, 3s. 6d. And in French morocco or Russia, 5s.
ESSAYS ON SOCIAL SUBJECTS. Originally published in the 'Saturday Review.' A New Edition. First and Second Series. 2 vols. crown 8vo, 6s. each.
EWALD. The Crown and its Advisers; or, Queen, Ministers, Lords, and Commons. By ALEXANDER CHARLES EWALD, F.S.A. Crown 8vo, 5s.
FAITHS OF THE WORLD, The. A Concise History of the Great Religious Systems of the World. By various Authors. Being the St Giles' Lectures—Second Series. Complete in one volume, crown 8vo, 5s
FARRER. A Tour in Greece in 1880. By RICHARD RIDLEY FARRER. With Twenty-seven full-page Illustrations by LORD WINDSOR. Royal 8vo, with a Map, 21s.
FAUCIT. Some of Shakespeare's Female Characters. In a Series of Letters. By HELENA FAUCIT, LADY MARTIN. With Portraits engraved by the late F. Holl. Dedicated by Special Permission to Her Most Gracious Majesty the Queen. 4to, printed on hand-made paper. 21s.
FERRIER. Philosophical Works of the late James F. Ferrier, B.A. Oxon., Professor of Moral Philosophy and Political Economy, St Andrews. New Edition. Edited by Sir ALEX. GRANT, Bart., D.C.L., and Professor LUSHINGTON. 3 vols. crown 8vo, 34s. 6d.
——— Institutes of Metaphysic. Third Edition. 10s. 6d.
——— Lectures on the Early Greek Philosophy. Third Edition, 10s. 6d.
——— Philosophical Remains, including the Lectures on Early Greek Philosophy. 2 vols., 24s.

FLETCHER. Lectures on the Opening Clauses of the Litany delivered in St Paul's Church, Edinburgh. By JOHN B. FLETCHER, M.A. Crown 8vo, 4s.

FLINT. The Philosophy of History in Europe. Vol. I., containing the History of that Philosophy in France and Germany. By ROBERT FLINT, D.D., LL.D., Professor of Divinity, University of Edinburgh. 8vo.
[*New Edition in preparation.*

——— Theism. Being the Baird Lecture for 1876. Fourth Edition. Crown 8vo, 7s. 6d.

——— Anti-Theistic Theories. Being the Baird Lecture for 1877. Third Edition. Crown 8vo, 10s. 6d.

FORBES. The Campaign of Garibaldi in the Two Sicilies : A Personal Narrative. By CHARLES STUART FORBES, Commander, R.N. Post 8vo, with Portraits, 12s.

FOREIGN CLASSICS FOR ENGLISH READERS. Edited by Mrs OLIPHANT. Price 2s. 6d. *For List of Volumes issued, see p.* 2.

FRANZOS. The Jews of Barnow. Stories by KARL EMIL FRANZOS. Translated by M. W. MACDOWALL. Crown 8vo, 6s.

GALT. Annals of the Parish. By JOHN GALT. Fcap. 8vo, 2s.

——— The Provost. Fcap. 8vo, 2s.

——— Sir Andrew Wylie. Fcap. 8vo, 2s.

——— The Entail ; or, The Laird of Grippy. Fcap. 8vo, 2s.

GENERAL ASSEMBLY OF THE CHURCH OF SCOTLAND.

——— Family Prayers. Authorised by the General Assembly of the Church of Scotland. A New Edition, crown 8vo, in large type, 4s. 6d. Another Edition, crown 8vo, 2s.

——— Prayers for Social and Family Worship. For the Use of Soldiers, Sailors, Colonists, and Sojourners in India, and other Persons, at home and abroad, who are deprived of the ordinary services of a Christian Ministry. Cheap Edition, 1s. 6d.

——— The Scottish Hymnal. Hymns for Public Worship. Published for Use in Churches by Authority of the General Assembly. Various sizes—viz. ; 1. Large type, for Pulpit use, cloth, 3s. 6d. 2. Longprimer type, cloth, red edges, 1s. 6d. ; French morocco, 2s. 6d. ; calf, 6s. 3. Bourgeois type, cloth, red edges, 1s. ; French morocco, 2s. 4. Minion type, limp cloth, 6d. ; French morocco, 1s. 6d. 5. School Edition, in paper cover, 2d. 6. Children's Hymnal, paper cover, 1d. No. 2, bound with the Psalms and Paraphrases, cloth, 3s. ; French morocco, 4s. 6d. ; calf, 7s. 6d. No. 3, bound with the Psalms and Paraphrases, cloth, 2s. ; French morocco, 3s.

——— The Scottish Hymnal, with Music. Selected by the Committees on Hymns and on Psalmody. The harmonies arranged by W. H. Monk. Cloth, 1s. 6d. ; French morocco, 3s. 6d. The same in the Tonic Sol-fa Notation, 1s. 6d. and 3s. 6d.

——— The Scottish Hymnal, with Fixed Tune for each Hymn. Longprimer type, 3s. 6d.

——— The Scottish Hymnal Appendix. 1. Longprimer type, 1s. 2. Nonpareil type, cloth limp, 4d. ; paper cover, 2d.

——— Scottish Hymnal with Appendix Incorporated. Bourgeois type, limp cloth, 1s. Large type, cloth, red edges, 2s. 6d. Nonpareil type, paper covers, 3d. ; cloth, red edges, 6d.

GERARD. Reata : What's in a Name. By E. D. GERARD. New Edition. In one volume, crown 8vo, 6s.

——— Beggar my Neighbour. New Edition. Crown 8vo, 6s.

——— The Waters of Hercules. 3 vols. Post 8vo, 25s. 6d.

GOETHE'S FAUST. Translated into English Verse by Sir THEO-
DORE MARTIN, K.C.B. Second Edition, post 8vo, 6s. Cheap Edition, fcap.,
3s. 6d.
GOETHE. Poems and Ballads of Goethe. Translated by Professor
AYTOUN and Sir THEODORE MARTIN, K.C.B. Third Edition, fcap. 8vo, 6s.
GORDON CUMMING. At Home in Fiji. By C. F. GORDON
CUMMING, Author of 'From the Hebrides to the Himalayas.' Fourth Edition,
post 8vo. With Illustrations and Map. 7s. 6d.
—— A Lady's Cruise in a French Man-of-War. New and
Cheaper Edition. 8vo. With Illustrations and Map. 12s. 6d.
—— Fire-Fountains. The Kingdom of Hawaii: Its Volcanoes,
and the History of its Missions. With Map and numerous Illustrations. 2
vols. 8vo, 25s.
—— Granite Crags: The Yō-semité Region of California. Illus-
trated with 8 Engravings. One vol. 8vo, 16s.
—— Wanderings in China. 2 vols. 8vo, with Illustrations.
[In the press.
GRAHAM. The Life and Work of Syed Ahmed Khan, C.S.I.
By Lieut.-Colonel G. F. I GRAHAM, B.S.C. In one vol. 8vo. [Immediately.
GRANT. Bush-Life in Queensland. By A. C. GRANT. New
Edition. Crown 8vo, 6s.
HAMERTON. Wenderholme: A Story of Lancashire and York-
shire Life. By PHILIP GILBERT HAMERTON, Author of 'A Painter's Camp.' A
New Edition. Crown 8vo, 6s.
HAMILTON. Lectures on Metaphysics. By Sir WILLIAM HAMIL-
TON, Bart., Professor of Logic and Metaphysics in the University of Edinburgh.
Edited by the Rev. H. L. MANSEL, B.D., LL.D., Dean of St Paul's; and JOHN
VEITCH, M.A., Professor of Logic and Rhetoric, Glasgow. Sixth Edition. 2
vols. 8vo, 24s.
—— Lectures on Logic. Edited by the SAME. Third Edition.
2 vols., 24s.
—— Discussions on Philosophy and Literature, Education and
University Reform. Third Edition, 8vo, 21s.
—— Memoir of Sir William Hamilton, Bart., Professor of Logic
and Metaphysics in the University of Edinburgh. By Professor VEITCH of the
University of Glasgow. 8vo, with Portrait, 18s.
—— Sir William Hamilton: The Man and his Philosophy.
Two Lectures Delivered before the Edinburgh Philosophical Institution,
January and February 1883. By the SAME. Crown 8vo, 2s.
HAMILTON. Annals of the Peninsular Campaigns. By Captain
THOMAS HAMILTON. Edited by F. Hardman. 8vo, 16s. Atlas of Maps to
illustrate the Campaigns, 12s.
HAMILTON. Mr Montenello. A Romance of the Civil Service.
By W. A. BAILLIE HAMILTON. In 3 vols. post 8vo, 25s. 6d
HAMLEY. The Operations of War Explained and Illustrated. By
Major-General Sir EDWARD BRUCE HAMLEY, K C.M.G. Fourth Edition,
revised throughout. 4to, with numerous Illustrations, 30s.
—— Thomas Carlyle: An Essay. Second Edition. Crown
8vo. 2s. 6d.
—— The Story of the Campaign of Sebastopol. Written in the
Camp. With Illustrations drawn in Camp by the Author. 8vo, 21s.
—— On Outposts. Second Edition. 8vo, 2s.
—— Wellington's Career; A Military and Political Summary.
Crown 8vo, 2s.
—— Lady Lee's Widowhood. Crown 8vo, 2s. 6d.
—— Our Poor Relations. A Philozoic Essay. With Illus-
trations, chiefly by Ernest Griset. Crown 8vo, cloth gilt, 3s. 6d.

HAMLEY. Guilty, or Not Guilty? A Tale. By Major-General W. G. HAMLEY, late of the Royal Engineers. New Edition. Crown 8vo, 3s. 6d.

—— Traseaden Hall. "When George the Third was King." New and Cheaper Edition, crown 8vo, 6s.

HARBORD. Definitions and Diagrams in Astronomy and Navigation. By the Rev. J. B. HARBORD, M.A., Assistant Director of Education, Admiralty. 1s.

—— Short Sermons for Hospitals and Sick Seamen. Fcap. 8vo, cloth, 4s. 6d.

HARDMAN. Scenes and Adventures in Central America. Edited by FREDERICK HARDMAN. Crown 8vo. 6s.

HARRISON. Oure Tounis Colledge. Sketches of the History of the Old College of Edinburgh, with an Appendix of Historical Documents. By JOHN HARRISON. Crown 8vo, 5s.

HASELL. Bible Partings. By E. J. HASELL. Crown 8vo, 6s.

—— Short Family Prayers. By Miss HASELL. Cloth, 1s.

HAY. The Works of the Right Rev. Dr George Hay, Bishop of Edinburgh. Edited under the Supervision of the Right Rev. Bishop STRAIN. With Memoir and Portrait of the Author. 5 vols. crown 8vo, bound in extra cloth, £1, 1s. Or, sold separately—viz.:

The Sincere Christian Instructed in the Faith of Christ from the Written Word. 2 vols., 8s.—The Devout Christian Instructed in the Law of Christ from the Written Word. 2 vols., 8s.—The Pious Christian Instructed in the Nature and Practice of the Principal Exercises of Piety. 1 vol., 4s.

HEATLEY. The Horse-Owner's Safeguard. A Handy Medical Guide for every Man who owns a Horse. By G. S. HEATLEY, M.R.C., V.S. Crown 8vo, 5s.

—— The Stock-Owner's Guide. A Handy Medical Treatise for every Man who owns an Ox or a Cow. Crown 8vo, 4s. 6d.

HEMANS. The Poetical Works of Mrs Hemans. Copyright Editions.—One Volume, royal 8vo, 5s.—The Same, with Illustrations engraved on Steel, bound in cloth, gilt edges, 7s. 6d.—Six Volumes in Three, fcap., 12s. 6d. SELECT POEMS OF MRS HEMANS. Fcap., cloth, gilt edges, 3s.

HOBART PACHA. The Torpedo Scare; Experiences during the Turco-Russian War. By HOBART PACHA. Reprinted from 'Blackwood's Magazine,' with additional matter. Crown 8vo., 1s.

HOLE. A Book about Roses: How to Grow and Show Them. By the Rev. Canon HOLE. Eighth and Cheaper Edition, revised. Crown 8vo, 3s. 6d.

HOME PRAYERS. By Ministers of the Church of Scotland and Members of the Church Service Society. Second Edition. Fcap. 8vo, 3s.

HOMER. The Odyssey. Translated into English Verse in the Spenserian Stanza. By PHILIP STANHOPE WORSLEY. Third Edition, 2 vols. fcap., 12s.

—— The Iliad. Translated by P. S. WORSLEY and Professor CONINGTON. 2 vols. crown 8vo, 21s.

HOSACK. Mary Queen of Scots and Her Accusers. Containing a Variety of Documents never before published. By JOHN HOSACK, Barrister-at-Law. A New and Enlarged Edition, with a Photograph from the Bust on the Tomb in Westminster Abbey. 2 vols. 8vo, £1, 1s.

HYDE. The Royal Mail; its Curiosities and Romance. By JAMES WILSON HYDE, Superintendent in the General Post Office, Edinburgh. Second Edition, enlarged. Crown 8vo, with Illustrations, 6s.

INDEX GEOGRAPHICUS: Being a List, alphabetically arranged, of the Principal Places on the Globe, with the Countries and Subdivisions of the Countries in which they are situated, and their Latitudes and Longitudes. Applicable to all Modern Atlases and Maps. Imperial 8vo, pp. 676, 21s.

JEAN JAMBON. Our Trip to Blunderland; or, Grand Excursion to Blundertown and Back. By JEAN JAMBON. With Sixty Illustrations designed by CHARLES DOYLE, engraved by DALZIEL. Fourth Thousand. Handsomely bound in cloth, gilt edges, 6s. 6d. Cheap Edition, cloth, 3s. 6d. In boards, 2s. 6d.

JOHNSON. The Scots Musical Museum. Consisting of upwards of Six Hundred Songs, with proper Basses for the Pianoforte. Originally published by JAMES JOHNSON; and now accompanied with Copious Notes and Illustrations of the Lyric Poetry and Music of Scotland, by the late WILLIAM STENHOUSE; with additional Notes and Illustrations, by DAVID LAING and C. K. SHARPE. 4 vols. 8vo, Roxburghe binding, £2, 12s. 6d.

JOHNSTON. The Chemistry of Common Life. By Professor J. F. W. JOHNSTON. New Edition, Revised, and brought down to date. By ARTHUR HERBERT CHURCH, M.A. OXON.; Author of 'Food: its Sources, Constituents, and Uses;' 'The Laboratory Guide for Agricultural Students;' 'Plain Words about Water,' &c. Illustrated with Maps and 102 Engravings on Wood. Complete in one volume, crown 8vo, pp. 618, 7s. 6d.

—— Elements of Agricultural Chemistry and Geology. Thirteenth Edition, Revised, and brought down to date. By Sir CHARLES A. CAMERON, M.D., F.R.C.S.I., &c. Feap. 8vo, 6s. 6d.

—— Catechism of Agricultural Chemistry and Geology. An entirely New Edition, revised and enlarged, by Sir CHARLES A. CAMERON, M.D., F.R.C.S.I., &c. Eighty-first Thousand, with numerous Illustrations, 1s.

JOHNSTON. Patrick Hamilton: a Tragedy of the Reformation in Scotland, 1528. By T. P. JOHNSTON. Crown 8vo, with Two Etchings by the Author, 5s.

KENNEDY. Sport, Travel, and Adventures in Newfoundland and the West Indies. By Captain W. R. KENNEDY, R.N. With Illustrations by the Author. Post 8vo, 14s.

KING. The Metamorphoses of Ovid. Translated in English Blank Verse. By HENRY KING, M.A., Fellow of Wadham College, Oxford, and of the Inner Temple, Barrister-at-Law. Crown 8vo, 10s. 6d.

KINGLAKE. History of the Invasion of the Crimea. By A. W. KINGLAKE. Cabinet Edition. Seven Volumes, crown 8vo, at 6s. each. The Volumes respectively contain:—
  I. THE ORIGIN OF THE WAR between the Czar and the Sultan.
  II. RUSSIA MET AND INVADED. With 4 Maps and Plans.
  III. THE BATTLE OF THE ALMA. With 14 Maps and Plans.
  IV. SEBASTOPOL AT BAY. With 10 Maps and Plans.
  V. THE BATTLE OF BALACLAVA. With 10 Maps and Plans.
  VI. THE BATTLE OF INKERMAN. With 11 Maps and Plans.
  VII. WINTER TROUBLES. With Map.

—— History of the Invasion of the Crimea. Vol. VI. Winter Troubles. Demy 8vo, with a Map, 16s.

—— History of the Invasion of the Crimea. Vol. VII. Demy 8vo. [In preparation.

—— Eothen. A New Edition, uniform with the Cabinet Edition of the 'History of the Crimean War,' price 6s.

KNOLLYS. The Elements of Field-Artillery. Designed for the Use of Infantry and Cavalry Officers. By HENRY KNOLLYS, Captain Royal Artillery; Author of 'From Sedan to Saarbrück,' Editor of 'Incidents in the Sepoy War,' &c. With Engravings. Crown 8vo, 7s. 6d.

LAING. Select Remains of the Ancient Popular and Romance Poetry of Scotland. Originally Collected and Edited by DAVID LAING, LL.D. Re-edited, with Memorial-Introduction, by JOHN SMALL, M.A. With a Portrait of Dr Laing. 4to, 25s. The Edition has been limited to 350 copies, and when one-half of the Edition is disposed of, the price will be increased.

LAVERGNE. The Rural Economy of England, Scotland, and Ireland. By LEONCE DE LAVERGNE. Translated from the French. With Notes by a Scottish Farmer. 8vo, 12s.

LEE. Lectures on the History of the Church of Scotland, from the Reformation to the Revolution Settlement. By the late Very Rev. JOHN LEE, D.D., LL.D., Principal of the University of Edinburgh. With Notes and Appendices from the Author's Papers. Edited by the Rev. WILLIAM LEE, D.D. 2 vols. 8vo, 21s.

LEE. Miss Brown: A Novel. By VERNON LEE. 3 vols. post 8vo, 25s. 6d.

LEE. Glimpses in the Twilight. Being various Notes, Records, and Examples of the Supernatural. By the Rev. GEORGE F. LEE, D.C.L. Crown 8vo. 8s. 6d.

LEE-HAMILTON. Poems and Transcripts. By EUGENE LEE-HAMILTON. Crown 8vo, 6s.

LEES. A Handbook of Sheriff Court Styles. By J. M. LEES, M.A., LL.B., Advocate, Sheriff-Substitute of Lanarkshire. 8vo, 16s.

—— A Handbook of the Sheriff and Justice of Peace Small Debt Courts. 8vo, 7s. 6d.

LETTERS FROM THE HIGHLANDS. Reprinted from 'The Times.' Fcap. 8vo, 4s. 6d.

LINDAU. The Philosopher's Pendulum and other Stories. By RUDOLPH LINDAU. Crown 8vo, 7s. 6d.

LITTLE. Madagascar: Its History and People. By the Rev. HENRY W. LITTLE, some years Missionary in East Madagascar. Post 8vo, 10s. 6d.

LOCKHART. Doubles and Quits. By LAURENCE W. M. LOCKHART. With Twelve Illustrations. Third Edition. Crown 8vo, 6s.

—— Fair to See: a Novel. Eighth Edition, crown 8vo, 6s.

—— Mine is Thine: a Novel. Seventh Edition, crown 8vo, 6s.

LORIMER. The Institutes of Law: A Treatise of the Principles of Jurisprudence as determined by Nature. By JAMES LORIMER, Regius Professor of Public Law and of the Law of Nature and Nations in the University of Edinburgh. New Edition, revised throughout, and much enlarged. 8vo, 18s.

—— The Institutes of the Law of Nations. A Treatise of the Jural Relation of Separate Political Communities. In 2 vols. 8vo. Volume I., price 16s. Volume II., price 20s.

M'COMBIE. Cattle and Cattle-Breeders. By WILLIAM M'COMBIE, Tillyfour. A New and Cheaper Edition, 2s. 6d., cloth.

MACRAE. A Handbook of Deer-Stalking. By ALEXANDER MACRAE, late Forester to Lord Henry Bentinck. With Introduction by HORATIO ROSS, Esq. Fcap. 8vo, with two Photographs from Life. 3s. 6d.

M'CRIE. Works of the Rev. Thomas M'Crie, D.D. Uniform Edition. Four vols. crown 8vo, 24s.

—— Life of John Knox. Containing Illustrations of the History of the Reformation in Scotland. Crown 8vo, 6s. Another Edition, 3s. 6d.

—— Life of Andrew Melville. Containing Illustrations of the Ecclesiastical and Literary History of Scotland in the Sixteenth and Seventeenth Centuries. Crown 8vo, 6s.

—— History of the Progress and Suppression of the Reformation in Italy in the Sixteenth Century. Crown 8vo, 4s.

—— History of the Progress and Suppression of the Reformation in Spain in the Sixteenth Century. Crown 8vo, 3s. 6d.

—— Lectures on the Book of Esther. Fcap. 8vo, 5s.

M'INTOSH. The Book of the Garden. By CHARLES M'INTOSH, formerly Curator of the Royal Gardens of his Majesty the King of the Belgians, and lately of those of his Grace the Duke of Buccleuch, K.G., at Dalkeith Palace. Two large vols. royal 8vo, embellished with 1350 Engravings. £4, 7s. 6d.
Vol. I. On the Formation of Gardens and Construction of Garden Edifices. 776 pages, and 1073 Engravings, £2, 10s.
Vol. II. Practical Gardening. 868 pages, and 279 Engravings, £1, 17s. 6d.

MACKAY. A Manual of Modern Geography; Mathematical, Physical, and Political. By the Rev. ALEXANDER MACKAY, LL.D., F.R.G.S. 11th Edition, revised to the present time. Crown 8vo, pp. 688. 7s. 6d.
—— Elements of Modern Geography. 51st Thousand, revised to the present time. Crown 8vo, pp. 300, 3s.
—— The Intermediate Geography. Intended as an Intermediate Book between the Author's 'Outlines of Geography' and 'Elements of Geography.' Tenth Edition, revised. Crown 8vo, pp. 224, 2s.
—— Outlines of Modern Geography. 170th Thousand, revised to the present time. 18mo, pp. 118, 1s.
—— First Steps in Geography. 82d Thousand. 18mo, pp. 56. Sewed, 4d.; cloth, 6d.
—— Elements of Physiography and Physical Geography. With Express Reference to the Instructions recently issued by the Science and Art Department. 25th Thousand, revised. Crown 8vo, 1s. 6d.
—— Facts and Dates; or, the Leading Events in Sacred and Profane History, and the Principal Facts in the various Physical Sciences. The Memory being aided throughout by a Simple and Natural Method. For Schools and Private Reference. New Edition. Crown 8vo, 3s. 6d.

MACKAY. An Old Scots Brigade. Being the History of Mackay's Regiment, now incorporated with the Royal Scots. With an Appendix containing many Original Documents connected with the History of the Regiment. By JOHN MACKAY (late) OF HERRIESDALE. Crown 8vo. [In the press.

MACKAY. The Founders of the American Republic. A History of Washington, Adams, Jefferson, Franklin, and Madison. With a Supplementary Chapter on the Inherent Causes of the Ultimate Failure of American Democracy. By CHARLES MACKAY, LL.D. Post 8vo, 10s. 6d.

MACKELLAR. More Leaves from the Journal of a Life in the Highlands, from 1862 to 1882. Translated into Gaelic by Mrs MARY MACKELLAR. By command of Her Majesty the Queen. In one vol. crown 8vo, with Illustrations. [In the press.

MACKENZIE. Studies in Roman Law. With Comparative Views of the Laws of France, England, and Scotland. By LORD MACKENZIE, one of the Judges of the Court of Session in Scotland. Fifth Edition, Edited by JOHN KIRKPATRICK, Esq., M.A. Cantab.; Dr Jur. Heidelb.; LL.B., Edin.; Advocate. 8vo, 12s.

MADOC. Thereby. A Novel. By FAYR MADOC. Two vols. Post 8vo, 17s.

MAIN. Three Hundred English Sonnets. Chosen and Edited by DAVID M. MAIN. Fcap. 8vo, 6s.

MANNERS. Notes of an Irish Tour in 1846. By Lord JOHN MANNERS, M.P., G.C.B. New Edition. Crown 8vo, 2s. 6d.

MANNERS. Gems of German Poetry. Translated by Lady JOHN MANNERS. Small quarto, 3s. 6d.
—— Impressions of Bad-Homburg. Comprising a Short Account of the Women's Associations of Germany under the Red Cross. By Lady JOHN MANNERS. Crown 8vo, 1s. 6d.
—— Some Personal Recollections of the Later Years of the Earl of Beaconsfield, K.G. Fifth Edition, 6d.

MANNERS. Employment of Women in the Public Service. By LADY JOHN MANNERS. 6d.

——— Some of the Advantages of Easily Accessible Reading and Recreation Rooms, and Free Libraries. With Remarks on Starting and Maintaining Them. Reprinted from 'The Queen.' Dedicated by Special Permission to Her Majesty the Queen. Crown 8vo, 1s.

——— A Sequel to Rich Men's Dwellings, and other Occasional Papers. In one vol. crown 8vo. [Shortly.

MARMORNE. The Story is told by ADOLPHUS SEGRAVE, the youngest of three Brothers. Third Edition. Crown 8vo, 6s.

MARSHALL. French Home Life. By FREDERIC MARSHALL. Second Edition. 5s.

MARSHMAN. History of India. From the Earliest Period to the Close of the India Company's Government; with an Epitome of Subsequent Events. By JOHN CLARK MARSHMAN, C.S.I. Abridged from the Author's larger work. Second Edition, revised. Crown 8vo, with Map, 6s. 6d.

MARTIN. Goethe's Faust. Translated by Sir THEODORE MARTIN, K.C.B. Second Edition, crown 8vo, 6s. Cheap Edition, 3s. 6d.

——— The Works of Horace. Translated into English Verse, with Life and Notes. In 2 vols. crown 8vo, printed on hand-made paper, 21s.

——— Poems and Ballads of Heinrich Heine. Done into English Verse. Second Edition. Printed on papier vergé, crown 8vo, 8s.

——— Catullus. With Life and Notes. Second Edition, post 8vo, 7s. 6d.

———. The Vita Nuova of Dante. With an Introduction and Notes. Second Edition, crown 8vo, 5s.

——— Aladdin : A Dramatic Poem. By ADAM OEHLENSCHLAEGER. Fcap. 8vo, 5s.

——— Correggio : A Tragedy. By OEHLENSCHLAEGER. With Notes. Fcap. 8vo, 3s.

——— King Rene's Daughter : A Danish Lyrical Drama. By HENRIK HERTZ. Second Edition, fcap., 2s. 6d.

MARTIN. Some of Shakespeare's Female Characters. In a Series of Letters. By HELENA FAUCIT, LADY MARTIN. With Portraits engraved by the late F. Holl. Dedicated by Special Permission to Her Most Gracious Majesty the Queen. 4to, printed on hand-made paper, 21s.

MATHESON. Can the Old Faith Live with the New ? or the Problem of Evolution and Revelation. By the Rev. GEORGE MATHESON, D.D., Innellan. Crown 8vo, 7s. 6d.

MEIKLEJOHN. An Old Educational Reformer—Dr Bell. By J. M. D. MEIKLEJOHN, M.A., Professor of the Theory, History, and Practice of Education in the University of St Andrews. Crown 8vo, 3s. 6d.

MICHEL. A Critical Inquiry into the Scottish Language. With the view of Illustrating the Rise and Progress of Civilisation in Scotland. By FRANCISQUE-MICHEL, F.S.A. Lond. and Scot., Correspondant de l'Institut de France, &c. In One handsome Quarto Volume, printed on hand-made paper, and appropriately bound in Roxburghe style. Price 66s.

MICHIE. The Larch : Being a Practical Treatise on its Culture and General Management. By CHRISTOPHER YOUNG MICHIE, Forester, Cullen House. Crown 8vo, with Illustrations. New and Cheaper Edition, enlarged, 5s.

MILLIONAIRE, THE. By LOUIS J. JENNINGS, Author of 'Field Paths and Green Lanes,' 'Rambles among the Hills,' &c. Second Edition. 3 vols. crown 8vo, 25s. 6d.

MILNE. The Problem of the Churchless and Poor in our Large Towns. With special reference to the Home Mission Work of the Church of Scotland. By the Rev. ROBT. MILNE, M A., Towie. Crown 8vo, 5s.

MINTO. A Manual of English Prose Literature, Biographical and Critical: designed mainly to show Characteristics of Style. By W. MINTO, M.A., Professor of Logic in the University of Aberdeen. Second Edition, revised. Crown 8vo, 7s. 6d.

—— Characteristics of English Poets, from Chaucer to Shirley. New Edition, revised. Crown 8vo, 7s. 6d.

MITCHELL. Biographies of Eminent Soldiers of the last Four Centuries. By Major-General JOHN MITCHELL, Author of 'Life of Wallenstein.' With a Memoir of the Author. 8vo, 9s.

MOIR. Life of Mansie Wauch, Tailor in Dalkeith. With 8 Illustrations on Steel, by the late GEORGE CRUIKSHANK. Crown 8vo, 3s. 6d. Another Edition, fcap. 8vo, 1s. 6d.

MOMERIE. Defects of Modern Christianity, and other Sermons. By the Rev. A. W. MOMERIE, M.A., D Sc., Professor of Logic and Metaphysics in King's College, London. New Edition. Crown 8vo, 5s.

—— The Basis of Religion. Being an Examination of Natural Religion. Crown 8vo. 2s. 6d.

—— The Origin of Evil, and other Sermons. Fourth Edition, enlarged. Crown 8vo, 5s.

—— Personality. The Beginning and End of Metaphysics, and a Necessary Assumption in all Positive Philosophy. Second Edition. Crown 8vo, 3s.

—— Agnosticism, and other Sermons. Crown 8vo, 6s.

MONTAGUE. Campaigning in South Africa. Reminiscences of an Officer in 1879. By Captain W. E. MONTAGUE, 94th Regiment, Author of 'Claude Meadowleigh,' &c. 8vo, 10s. 6d.

MONTALEMBERT. Memoir of Count de Montalembert. A Chapter of Recent French History. By Mrs OLIPHANT, Author of the 'Life of Edward Irving,' &c. 2 vols. crown 8vo, £1, 4s.

MURDOCH. Manual of the Law of Insolvency and Bankruptcy: Comprehending a Summary of the Law of Insolvency, Notour Bankruptcy, Composition-contracts, Trust-deeds, Cessios, and Sequestrations; and the Winding-up of Joint-Stock Companies in Scotland; with Annotations on the various Insolvency and Bankruptcy Statutes; and with Forms of Procedure applicable to these Subjects. By JAMES MURDOCH, Member of the Faculty of Procurators in Glasgow. Fourth Edition, Revised and Enlarged, 8vo, £1.

MY TRIVIAL LIFE AND MISFORTUNE: A Gossip with no Plot in Particular By A PLAIN WOMAN. New Edition, crown 8vo, 6s.

NASEBY. Oaks and Birches. A Novel. By NASEBY. 3 vols. crown 8vo, 25s. 6d.

NEAVES. Songs and Verses, Social and Scientific. By an Old Contributor to 'Maga.' By the Hon. Lord NEAVES. Fifth Edition, fcap. 8vo, 4s.

—— The Greek Anthology. Being Vol. XX. of 'Ancient Classics for English Readers.' Crown 8vo, 2s. 6d.

NICHOLSON. A Manual of Zoology, for the Use of Students. With a General Introduction on the Principles of Zoology. By HENRY ALLEYNE NICHOLSON, M.D., D.Sc., F.L.S., F.G.S., Regius Professor of Natural History in the University of Aberdeen. Sixth Edition, revised and enlarged. Crown 8vo, pp. 816, with 394 Engravings on Wood, 14s.

—— Text-Book of Zoology, for the Use of Schools. Third Edition, enlarged. Crown 8vo, with 188 Engravings on Wood, 6s.

—— Introductory Text-Book of Zoology, for the Use of Junior Classes. Fifth Edition, revised and enlarged, with 156 Engravings, 3s.

—— Outlines of Natural History, for Beginners; being Descriptions of a Progressive Series of Zoological Types. Third Edition, with Engravings, 1s. 6d.

—— A Manual of Palæontology, for the Use of Students. With a General Introduction on the Principles of Palæontology. Second Edition. Revised and greatly enlarged. 2 vols. 8vo, with 722 Engravings, £2, 2s.

NICHOLSON. The Ancient Life-History of the Earth. An Outline of the Principles and Leading Facts of Palæontological Science. By HENRY ALLEYNE NICHOLSON, M.D., D.Sc , F.L.S., F G S , Regius Professor of Natural History in the University of Aberdeen. Crown 8vo, with numerous Engravings, 10s. 6d.

—— On the "Tabulate Corals" of the Palæozoic Period, with Critical Descriptions of Illustrative Species. Illustrated with 15 Lithograph Plates and numerous Engravings. Super-royal 8vo, 21s.

—— On the Structure and Affinities of the Genus Monticulipora and its Sub-Genera, with Critical Descriptions of Illustrative Species. Illustrated with numerous Engravings on wood and lithographed Plates. Super-royal 8vo, 18s.

—— Synopsis of the Classification of the Animal Kingdom 8vo, with 106 Illustrations, 6s.

NICHOLSON. Communion with Heaven, and other Sermons. By the late MAXWELL NICHOLSON, D.D., Minister of St Stephen's, Edinburgh. Crown 8vo, 5s. 6d.

—— Rest in Jesus. Sixth Edition. Fcap. 8vo, 4s. 6d.

OLIPHANT. The Land of Gilead. With Excursions in the Lebanon. By LAURENCE OLIPHANT, Author of 'Lord Elgin's Mission to China and Japan,' &c. With Illustrations and Maps. Demy 8vo, 21s.

—— The Land of Khemi. Post 8vo, with Illustrations, 10s. 6d.

—— Sympneumata: or, Evolutionary Functions now Active in Man Post 8vo, 10s. 6d.

—— Altiora Peto. Seventh Edition, Illustrated. Crown 8vo, 6s.

—— Traits and Travesties; Social and Political. Post 8vo, 10s. 6d.

—— Piccadilly: A Fragment of Contemporary Biography. With Eight Illustrations by Richard Doyle. Fifth Edition, 4s. 6d. Cheap Edition, in paper cover, 2s. 6d.

OLIPHANT. The Ladies Lindores. By Mrs OLIPHANT. 3 vols., 25s. 6d.

—— The Story of Valentine; and his Brother. 5s., cloth.

—— Katie Stewart. 2s. 6d.

—— Salem Chapel. 2s. 6d., cloth.

—— The Perpetual Curate. 2s. 6d., cloth.

—— Miss Marjoribanks. 2s. 6d., cloth.

—— The Rector, and the Doctor's Family. 1s. 6d., cloth.

—— John: A Love Story. 2s. 6d., cloth.

OSBORN. Narratives of Voyage and Adventure. By Admiral SHERARD OSBORN, C.B. 3 vols. crown 8vo, 12s.

OSSIAN. The Poems of Ossian in the Original Gaelic. With a Literal Translation into English, and a Dissertation on the Authenticity of the Poems. By the Rev. ARCHIBALD CLERK. 2 vols. imperial 8vo, £1, 11s. 6d.

OSWALD. By Fell and Fjord; or, Scenes and Studies in Iceland. By E. J. OSWALD. Post 8vo, with Illustrations. 7s. 6d.

PAGE. Introductory Text-Book of Geology. By DAVID PAGE, LL.D., Professor of Geology in the Durham University of Physical Science, Newcastle. With Engravings on Wood and Glossarial Index. Eleventh Edition, 2s. 6d.

—— Advanced Text-Book of Geology, Descriptive and Industrial. With Engravings, and Glossary of Scientific Terms. Sixth Edition, revised and enlarged, 7s. 6d.

—— Geology for General Readers. A Series of Popular Sketches in Geology and Palæontology. Third Edition, enlarged, 6s.

—— Introductory Text-Book of Physical Geography. With Sketch-Maps and Illustrations. Edited by CHARLES LAPWORTH, F.G.S., &c., Professor of Geology and Mineralogy in the Mason Science College, Birmingham. 11th Edition. 2s. 6d.

PAGE. Advanced Text-Book of Physical Geography. By DAVID
PAGE, LL.D., Professor of Geology in the Durham University of Physical
Science, Newcastle. Third Edition, Revised and Enlarged by Professor LAP-
WORTH. With Engravings. 5s.

PATON. Spindrift. By Sir J. NOEL PATON. Fcap., cloth, 5s.

—— Poems by a Painter. Fcap., cloth, 5s.

PATTERSON. Essays in History and Art. By R. HOGARTH
PATTERSON. 8vo, 12s.

—— The New Golden Age, and Influence of the Precious Metals
upon the World. 2 vols. 8vo, 31s. 6d.

PAUL. History of the Royal Company of Archers, the Queen's
Body-Guard for Scotland. By JAMES BALFOUR PAUL, Advocate of the Scottish
Bar. Crown 4to, with Portraits and other Illustrations. £2, 2s.

PAUL. Analysis and Critical Interpretation of the Hebrew Text of
the Book of Genesis. Preceded by a Hebrew Grammar, and Dissertations on
the Genuineness of the Pentateuch, and on the Structure of the Hebrew Language. By the Rev. WILLIAM PAUL, A.M. 8vo, 18s.

PETTIGREW. The Handy Book of Bees, and their Profitable
Management. By A. PETTIGREW. Fourth Edition, Enlarged, with Engravings. Crown 8vo, 3s. 6d.

PHILOSOPHICAL CLASSICS FOR ENGLISH READERS.
Companion Series to Ancient and Foreign Classics for English Readers.
Edited by WILLIAM KNIGHT, LL.D., Professor of Moral Philosophy, Uni-
versity of St Andrews. In crown 8vo volumes, with portraits, price 3s. 6d.

1. DESCARTES. By Professor Mahaffy, Dublin.
2. BUTLER. By the Rev. W. Lucas Collins, M.A., Honorary Canon of Peterborough.
3. BERKELEY. By Professor A. Campbell Fraser, Edinburgh.
4. FICHTE. By Professor Adamson, Owens College, Manchester.
5. KANT. By Professor Wallace, Oxford.
6. HAMILTON. By Professor Veitch, Glasgow.
7. HEGEL. By Professor Edward Caird, Glasgow.
8. LEIBNIZ. By J. Theodore Merz.
9. VICO. By Professor Flint, Edinburgh.
10. HOBBES. By Professor Croom Robertson, London.

POLLOK. The Course of Time : A Poem. By ROBERT POLLOK,
A.M. Small fcap. 8vo, cloth gilt, 2s. 6d. The Cottage Edition, 32mo, sewed,
8d. The Same, cloth, gilt edges, 1s. 6d. Another Edition, with Illustrations
by Birket Foster and others, fcap., gilt cloth, 3s. 6d., or with edges gilt, 4s.

PORT ROYAL LOGIC. Translated from the French : with Introduction, Notes, and Appendix. By THOMAS SPENCER BAYNES, LL.D., Professor in the University of St Andrews. Eighth Edition, 12mo, 4s.

POST-MORTEM. Third Edition, 1s.

BY THE SAME AUTHOR.

The Autobiography of Thomas Allen. 3 vols. post 8vo,
25s. 6d.

The Apparition. Crown 8vo, with Frontispiece, 5s.

Simiocracy: A Fragment from Future History. Crown 8vo.
1s. 6d.

POTTS AND DARNELL. Aditus Faciliores: An easy Latin Con-
struing Book, with Complete Vocabulary. By A. W. POTTS, M.A., LL.D.,
Head-Master of the Fettes College, Edinburgh, and sometime Fellow of St
John's College, Cambridge; and the Rev. C. DARNELL, M.A., Head-Master of
Cargilfield Preparatory School, Edinburgh, and late Scholar of Pembroke and
Downing Colleges, Cambridge. Eighth Edition, fcap. 8vo, 3s. 6d.

—— Aditus Faciliores Graeci. An easy Greek Construing Book,
with Complete Vocabulary. Third Edition, fcap. 8vo, 3s.

PRINGLE. The Live-Stock of the Farm. By ROBERT O. PRINGLE.
Third Edition, crown 8vo. [In the press.

PRINGLE. Towards the Mountains of the Moon. A Journey in
East Africa. By Mrs Pringle of Whytbank, Yair. With a Map, 8vo, 12s. 6d.

PUBLIC GENERAL STATUTES AFFECTING SCOTLAND, from 1707 to 1847, with Chronological Table and Index. 3 vols. large 8vo, £3, 3s.

PUBLIC GENERAL STATUTES AFFECTING SCOTLAND, COLLECTION OF. Published Annually with General Index.

RAMSAY. Rough Recollections of Military Service and Society. By Lieut.-Col. BALCARRES D. WARDLAW RAMSAY. Two vols. post 8vo, 21s.

RANKINE. A Treatise on the Rights and Burdens incident to the Ownership of Lands and other Heritages in Scotland. By JOHN RANKINE, M.A., Advocate. Second Edition, Revised and Enlarged. In One large Volume, 8vo, 45s.

RECORDS OF THE TERCENTENARY FESTIVAL OF THE UNIVERSITY OF EDINBURGH. Celebrated in April 1884. Published under the Sanction of the Senatus Academicus. Large 4to, £2, 12s. 6d. *Only 150 copies printed for sale to the public.*

REID. A Handy Manual of German Literature. By M. F. REID. For Schools, Civil Service Competitions, and University Local Examinations. Fcap. 8vo, 3s.

RIMMER. The Early Homes of Prince Albert. By ALFRED RIMMER, Author of 'Our Old Country Towns,' &c. Beautifully Illustrated with Tinted Plates and numerous Engravings on Wood. 8vo, 21s.

ROBERTSON. Orellana, and other Poems. By J. LOGIE ROBERTSON. Fcap. 8vo. Printed on hand-made paper. 6s.

——— Our Holiday Among the Hills. By JAMES and JANET LOGIE ROBERTSON. Fcap. 8vo, 3s. 6d.

ROSCOE. Rambles with a Fishing-rod. By E. S. ROSCOE. Crown 8vo, 4s. 6d.

ROSS. Old Scottish Regimental Colours. By ANDREW ROSS, S S.C., Hon. Secretary Old Scottish Regimental Colours Committee. Dedicated by Special Permission to Her Majesty the Queen. In one vol. folio, handsomely bound in cloth, £2, 12s. 6d.

RUSSELL. The Haigs of Bemersyde. A Family History. By JOHN RUSSELL. Large octavo, with Illustrations. 21s.

RUSTOW. The War for the Rhine Frontier, 1870 : Its Political and Military History. By Col. W. RUSTOW. Translated from the German, by JOHN LAYLAND NEEDHAM, Lieutenant R.M. Artillery. 3 vols. 8vo, with Maps and Plans, £1, 11s. 6d.

SCHETKY. Ninety Years of Work and Play. Sketches from the Public and Private Career of JOHN CHRISTIAN SCHETKY, late Marine Painter in Ordinary to the Queen. By his DAUGHTER. Crown 8vo, 7s. 6d

SCOTCH LOCH FISHING. By "Black Palmer." Crown 8vo, interleaved with blank pages, 4s.

SELLER AND STEPHENS. Physiology at the Farm ; in Aid of Rearing and Feeding the Live Stock. By WILLIAM SELLER, M.D., F.R.S.E., Fellow of the Royal College of Physicians, Edinburgh, formerly Lecturer on Materia Medica and Dietetics ; and HENRY STEPHENS, F.R.S.E., Author of 'The Book of the Farm,' &c. Post 8vo, with Engravings, 16s.

SETON. Memoir of Alexander Seton, Earl of Dunfermline, Seventh President of the Court of Session, and Lord Chancellor of Scotland. By GEORGE SETON, M.A. Oxon.; Author of the 'Law and Practice of Heraldry in Scotland,' &c. Crown 4to, 42s.

SHADWELL. The Life of Colin Campbell, Lord Clyde. Illustrated by Extracts from his Diary and Correspondence. By Lieutenant-General SHADWELL, C.B. 2 vols. 8vo. With Portrait, Maps, and Plans. 36s.

SHAND. Letters from the West of Ireland. Reprinted from the 'Times.' By ALEXANDER INNES SHAND, Author of 'Letters from the West Highlands.' Crown 8vo, 5s.

SIM. Margaret Sim's Cookery. With an Introduction by L. B. WALFORD, Author of 'Mr Smith : A Part of His Life,' &c. Crown 8vo, 5s

SIMPSON. Dogs of other Days : Nelson and Puck. By EVE BLANTYRE SIMPSON. Fcap. 8vo, with Illustrations, 2s. 6d.

SMITH. Italian Irrigation: A Report on the Agricultural Canals of Piedmont and Lombardy, addressed to the Hon. the Directors of the East India Company; with an Appendix, containing a Sketch of the Irrigation System of Northern and Central India. By Lieut.-Col. R. Baird Smith, F.G.S., Captain, Bengal Engineers. Second Edition. 2 vols. 8vo, with Atlas in folio, 30s.

SMITH. Thorndale; or, The Conflict of Opinions. By William Smith, Author of 'A Discourse on Ethics,' &c. A New Edition. Crown 8vo, 10s. 6d.

——— Gravenhurst; or, Thoughts on Good and Evil. Second Edition, with Memoir of the Author. Crown 8vo, 8s.

——— A Discourse on Ethics of the School of Paley. 8vo, 4s.

——— Dramas. 1. Sir William Crichton. 2. Athelwold. 3. Guidone. 24mo, boards, 3s.

SMITH. Greek Testament Lessons for Colleges, Schools, and Private Students, consisting chiefly of the Sermon on the Mount and the Parables of our Lord. With Notes and Essays. By the Rev. J. Hunter Smith, M.A., First Assistant Master at King Edward's School, Birmingham. Crown 8vo, 6s.

SMITH. Writings by the Way. By John Campbell Smith, M.A., Advocate. Crown 8vo, 9s.

SOLTERA. A Lady's Ride Across Spanish Honduras. By Maria Soltera. With Illustrations. Post 8vo, 12s. 6d.

SOUTHEY. The Birthday, and other Poems. Second Edition, 5s.

——— Chapters on Churchyards. Fcap., 2s. 6d.

SPEEDY. Sport in the Highlands and Lowlands of Scotland with Rod and Gun. By T. Speedy. 8vo, with Illustrations, 15s.

SPEKE. What led to the Discovery of the Nile Source. By John Hanning Speke, Captain H.M. Indian Army. 8vo, with Maps, &c., 14s.

SPROTT. The Worship and Offices of the Church of Scotland; or, the Celebration of Public Worship, the Administration of the Sacraments, and other Divine Offices, according to the Order of the Church of Scotland. By George W. Sprott, D.D., Minister of North Berwick. Crown 8vo, 6s.

STARFORTH. Villa Residences and Farm Architecture: A Series of Designs. By John Starforth, Architect. 102 Engravings. Second Edition, medium 4to, £2, 17s. 6d.

STATISTICAL ACCOUNT OF SCOTLAND. Complete, with Index, 15 vols. 8vo, £16, 16s.
Each County sold separately, with Title, Index, and Map, neatly bound in cloth, forming a very valuable Manual to the Landowner, the Tenant, the Manufacturer, the Naturalist, the Tourist, &c.

STEPHENS. The Book of the Farm; detailing the Labours of the Farmer, Farm-Steward, Ploughman, Shepherd, Hedger, Farm-Labourer, Field-Worker, and Cattleman. By Henry Stephens, F.R.S.E. Illustrated with Portraits of Animals painted from the life; and with 557 Engravings on Wood, representing the principal Field Operations, Implements, and Animals treated of in the Work. A New and Revised Edition, the third, in great part Rewritten. 2 vols. large 8vo, £2, 10s.

——— The Book of Farm Buildings; their Arrangement and Construction. By Henry Stephens, F.R.S.E., Author of 'The Book of the Farm;' and Robert Scott Burn. Illustrated with 1045 Plates and Engravings. Large 8vo, uniform with 'The Book of the Farm,' &c. £1, 11s. 6d.

——— The Book of Farm Implements and Machines. By J. Slight and R. Scott Burn, Engineers. Edited by Henry Stephens. Large 8vo, uniform with 'The Book of the Farm,' £2, 2s.

——— Catechism of Practical Agriculture. With Engravings. 1s.

STEWART. Advice to Purchasers of Horses. By John Stewart, V.S., Author of 'Stable Economy.' 2s. 6d.

——— Stable Economy. A Treatise on the Management of Horses in relation to Stabling, Grooming, Feeding, Watering, and Working. Seventh Edition, fcap. 8vo, 6s. 6d.

STONE. Hugh Moore: a Novel. By EVELYN STONE. 2 vols. crown 8vo, 17s.

STORMONTH. Etymological and Pronouncing Dictionary of the English Language. Including a very Copious Selection of Scientific Terms. For Use in Schools and Colleges, and as a Book of General Reference. By the Rev. JAMES STORMONTH. The Pronunciation carefully Revised by the Rev. P. H. PHELP, M.A. Cantab. Eighth Edition, Revised throughout, containing many words not to be found in any other Dictionary. Crown 8vo, pp. 800. 7s. 6d.

——— Dictionary of the English Language, Pronouncing, Etymological, and Explanatory. Revised by the Rev. P. H. PHELP. Library Edition. Imperial 8vo, handsomely bound in half morocco, 31s. 6d.

——— The School Etymological Dictionary and Word-Book. Combining the advantages of an ordinary pronouncing School Dictionary and an Etymological Spelling-book. Fcap. 8vo, pp. 254. 2s.

STORY. Nero; A Historical Play. By W. W. STORY, Author of 'Roba di Roma.' Fcap. 8vo, 6s.

——— Vallombrosa. Post 8vo, 5s.

——— He and She; or, A Poet's Portfolio. Fcap. 8vo, in parchment, 3s. 6d.

STRICKLAND. Lives of the Queens of Scotland, and English Princesses connected with the Regal Succession of Great Britain. By AGNES STRICKLAND. With Portraits and Historical Vignettes. 8 vols. post 8vo, £4, 4s.

STURGIS. John-a-Dreams. A Tale. By JULIAN STURGIS. New Edition, crown 8vo, 3s. 6d.

——— Little Comedies, Old and New. Crown 8vo, 7s. 6d.

SUTHERLAND. Handbook of Hardy Herbaceous and Alpine Flowers, for general Garden Decoration. Containing Descriptions, in Plain Language, of upwards of 1000 Species of Ornamental Hardy Perennial and Alpine Plants, adapted to all classes of Flower-Gardens, Rockwork, and Waters; along with Concise and Plain Instructions for their Propagation and Culture. By WILLIAM SUTHERLAND, Gardener to the Earl of Minto; formerly Manager of the Herbaceous Department at Kew. Crown 8vo, 7s. 6d.

TAYLOR. Destruction and Reconstruction: Personal Experiences of the Late War in the United States. By RICHARD TAYLOR, Lieutenant-General in the Confederate Army. 8vo, 10s. 6d.

TAYLOR. The Story of My Life. By the late Colonel MEADOWS TAYLOR, Author of 'The Confessions of a Thug,' &c. &c. Edited by his Daughter. New and cheaper Edition, being the Fourth. Crown 8vo, 6s.

TEMPLE. Lancelot Ward, M.P. A Love-Story. By GEORGE TEMPLE. Crown 8vo. 7s. 6d.

THOLUCK. Hours of Christian Devotion. Translated from the German of A. Tholuck, D.D., Professor of Theology in the University of Halle. By the Rev. ROBERT MENZIES, D.D. With a Preface written for this Translation by the Author. Second Edition, crown 8vo, 7s. 6d.

THOMSON. Handy Book of the Flower-Garden: being Practical Directions for the Propagation, Culture, and Arrangement of Plants in Flower-Gardens all the year round. Embracing all classes of Gardens, from the largest to the smallest. With Engraved and Coloured Plans, illustrative of the various systems of Grouping in Beds and Borders. By DAVID THOMSON, Gardener to his Grace the Duke of Buccleuch, K.G., at Drumlanrig. Third Edition, crown 8vo, 7s. 6d.

——— The Handy Book of Fruit-Culture under Glass: being a series of Elaborate Practical Treatises on the Cultivation and Forcing of Pines, Vines, Peaches, Figs, Melons, Strawberries, and Cucumbers. With Engravings of Hothouses, &c., most suitable for the Cultivation and Forcing of these Fruits. Second Edition. Crown 8vo, with Engravings, 7s. 6d.

THOMSON. A Practical Treatise on the Cultivation of the Grape-Vine. By WILLIAM THOMSON, Tweed Vineyards. Tenth Edition, 8vo, 5s.

TOM CRINGLE'S LOG. A New Edition, with Illustrations. Crown 8vo, cloth gilt, 5s. Cheap Edition, 2s.

TRAILL. Recaptured Rhymes. Being a Batch of Political and other Fugitives arrested and brought to Book. By H. D. TRAILL. Crown 8vo, 5s.

TRANSACTIONS OF THE HIGHLAND AND AGRICULTURAL SOCIETY OF SCOTLAND. Published annually, price 5s.

TROLLOPE. An Autobiography by Anthony Trollope. Two Volumes, post 8vo, with Portrait. Second Edition. Price 21s.

—— The Fixed Period. 2 vols. fcap. 8vo, 12s.

—— An Old Man's Love. 2 vols. crown 8vo, 12s.

TULLOCH. Rational Theology and Christian Philosophy in England in the Seventeenth Century. By JOHN TULLOCH, D.D., Principal of St Mary's College in the University of St Andrews; and one of her Majesty's Chaplains in Ordinary in Scotland. Second Edition. 2 vols. 8vo, 28s.

—— Modern Theories in Philosophy and Religion. 8vo, 15s.

—— The Christian Doctrine of Sin ; being the Croall Lecture for 1876. Crown 8vo, 6s.

—— Theism. The Witness of Reason and Nature to an All-Wise and Beneficent Creator. 8vo. 10s. 6d.

—— Luther, and other Leaders of the Reformation. Third Edition, enlarged. Crown 8vo, 7s. 6d.

TWO STORIES OF THE SEEN AND THE UNSEEN. 'THE OPEN DOOR,' 'OLD LADY MARY.' Crown 8vo, cloth, 2s. 6d.

VEITCH. Institutes of Logic. By JOHN VEITCH, LL.D., Professor of Logic and Rhetoric in the University of Glasgow. Post 8vo.
*[In the press.*

VIRGIL. The Æneid of Virgil. Translated in English Blank Verse by G. K. RICKARDS, M.A., and Lord RAVENSWORTH. 2 vols. fcap. 8vo, 10s.

WALFORD. The Novels of L. B. WALFORD. New and Uniform Edition. Crown 8vo, each 5s.

| MR SMITH: A PART OF HIS LIFE. | TROUBLESOME DAUGHTERS. |
| COUSINS. | DICK NETHERBY. |
| PAULINE. | THE BABY'S GRANDMOTHER. |

—— Nan, and other Stories. 2 vols. crown 8vo, 12s.

WARDEN. Poems. By FRANCIS HEYWOOD WARDEN. With a Notice by Dr Vanroth. Crown 8vo, 5s.

WARREN'S (SAMUEL) WORKS. People's Edition, 4 vols. crown 8vo, cloth, 15s. 6d. Or separately:—
Diary of a Late Physician. Cloth, 2s. 6d.; boards, 2s. Illustrated, crown 8vo, 7s 6d.
Ten Thousand A-Year. Cloth, 3s. 6d.; boards, 2s. 6d.
Now and Then. The Lily and the Bee. Intellectual and Moral Development of the Present Age. 4s. 6d.
Essays: Critical, Imaginative, and Juridical. 5s.

WARREN. The Five Books of the Psalms. With Marginal Notes. By Rev. SAMUEL L. WARREN, Rector of Esher, Surrey; late Fellow, Dean, and Divinity Lecturer, Wadham College, Oxford. Crown 8vo, 5s.

WATSON. Christ's Authority; and other Sermons. By the late ARCHIBALD WATSON, D.D., Minister of the Parish of Dundee, and one of Her Majesty's Chaplains for Scotland. With Introduction by the Very Rev. PRINCIPAL CAIRD, Glasgow. Crown 8vo, 7s. 6d.

WEBSTER. The Angler and the Loop-Rod. By DAVID WEBSTER. Crown 8vo, with Illustrations, 7s. 6d.

WELLINGTON. Wellington Prize Essays on "the System of Field Manœuvres best adapted for enabling our Troops to meet a Continental Army." Edited by Major-General Sir EDWARD BRUCE HAMLEY, K.C.M.G. 8vo, 12s. 6d.

WESTMINSTER ASSEMBLY. Minutes of the Westminster Assembly, while engaged in preparing their Directory for Church Government, Confession of Faith, and Catechisms (November 1644 to March 1649). Edited by the Rev. Professor ALEX. T. MITCHELL, of St Andrews, and the Rev. JOHN STRUTHERS, LL.D. With a Historical and Critical Introduction by Professor Mitchell. 8vo, 15s.

WHITE. The Eighteen Christian Centuries. By the Rev. JAMES WHITE, Author of 'The History of France.' Seventh Edition, post 8vo, with Index, 6s.

———— History of France, from the Earliest Times. Sixth Thousand, post 8vo, with Index, 6s.

WHITE. Archæological Sketches in Scotland—Kintyre and Knapdale. By Captain T. P. WHITE, R.E., of the Ordnance Survey. With numerous Illustrations. 2 vols. folio, £4, 4s. Vol. I., Kintyre, sold separately, £2, 2s.

WILLS AND GREENE. Drawing-room Dramas for Children. By W. G. WILLS and the Hon. Mrs GREENE. Crown 8vo, 6s.

WILSON. Works of Professor Wilson. Edited by his Son-in-Law Professor FERRIER. 12 vols. crown 8vo, £2, 8s.

———— Christopher in his Sporting-Jacket. 2 vols., 8s.

———— Isle of Palms, City of the Plague, and other Poems. 4s.

———— Lights and Shadows of Scottish Life, and other Tales. 4s.

———— Essays, Critical and Imaginative. 4 vols., 16s.

———— The Noctes Ambrosianæ. Complete, 4 vols., 14s.

———— The Comedy of the Noctes Ambrosianæ. By CHRISTOPHER NORTH. Edited by JOHN SKELTON, Advocate. With a Portrait of Professor Wilson and of the Ettrick Shepherd, engraved on Steel. Crown 8vo, 7s. 6d.

———— Homer and his Translators, and the Greek Drama. Crown 8vo, 4s.

WINGATE. Annie Weir, and other Poems. By DAVID WINGATE. Fcap. 8vo, 5s.

———— Lily Neil. A Poem. Crown 8vo, 4s. 6d.

WORDSWORTH. The Historical Plays of Shakspeare. With Introductions and Notes. By CHARLES WORDSWORTH, D.C.L., Bishop of S. Andrews. 3 vols. post 8vo, each price 7s. 6d.

———— A Discourse on Scottish Church History. From the Reformation to the Present Time. With Prefatory Remarks on the St Giles' Lectures, and Appendix of Notes and References. Crown 8vo, cloth, 2s. 6d

WORSLEY. Poems and Translations. By PHILIP STANHOPE WORSLEY, M.A. Edited by EDWARD WORSLEY. Second Edition, enlarged. Fcap. 8vo, 6s.

WYLDE. An Ill-Regulated Mind. A Novel. By KATHARINE WYLDE, Author of 'A Dreamer.' Crown 8vo, 7s. 6d.

YOUNG. Songs of Béranger done into English Verse. By WILLIAM YOUNG. New Edition, revised. Fcap. 8vo, 4s. 6d.

YULE. Fortification: for the Use of Officers in the Army, and Readers of Military History. By Col. YULE, Bengal Engineers. 8vo, with numerous Illustrations, 10s. 6d.

www.ingramcontent.com/pod-product-compliance
Lightning Source LLC
Chambersburg PA
CBHW021409230426
43666CB00006B/687